Praise for Charlotte Amelia Poe's work

Winner, Spectrum Art Prize, 2018

'Raw and remarkable.'
—*The Guardian*

'Shows us both the desperate and bleak angle to autism,
as well as the beautiful side.'
—Professor Simon Baron-Cohen

'A passionate, hugely articulate argument for the
acceptance of difference. Every teacher, every parent,
every person should read this book.'
—Meg Rosoff, author of *How I Live Now*

'Charlotte has the rare ability to take you on the most
incredible journey from the depths of despair to
laughing out loud.'
—Mary Simpson, Chief Executive, Spectrum

'Charlotte's unique and powerful account is of immense
personal and political value. Experience and expertise come
together with shocking generosity.
This is a guide for our times.'
—Sacha Craddock, art critic, writer and curator

HOW
TO BE
AUTISTIC

CHARLOTTE
AMELIA
POE

myriad m∞

First published in 2019 by
Myriad Editions
www.myriadeditions.com

Myriad Editions
An imprint of New Internationalist Publications
The Old Music Hall, 106–108 Cowley Rd, Oxford OX4 1JE

First printing
1 3 5 7 9 10 8 6 4 2

A CIP catalogue record for this book
is available from the British Library

ISBN (pbk) 978-1-912408-32-0
ISBN (ebk) 978-1-912408-33-7

Designed and typeset in Palatino
by New Internationalist, Oxford

Printed and bound in Great Britain
by Clays Ltd, Elcograf S.p.A

For M,
Because you were there at the lowest points,
you deserve this high point.
Okay?
xx

For E, E, R & R,
I hope you never, for a single second, doubt that
I have loved you every day of your lives.

xx

Contents

I must now unmake,
And rebuild.

how to be autistic

you will be told you are a troublemaker, that the thing you can't put into words yet that divorces you from everyone else is responsible for the way the other kids pick on you and you really must try harder to fit in. you will realise quickly that you cannot trust anybody, not really, because they will ask you to do things that break you, that will haunt you for years. you will meet people who you will revisit in nightmares and go to places that will hide behind your closed eyelids as you toss and turn at night. you will learn to be afraid. you will learn how to be afraid and still breathe. you will learn fear as survival.

nobody will ever tell you what is wrong with you, just that you are wrong, and that what you do and say is wrong. you will look at the world and you will see everybody else and find yourself lacking, and not know why. you will cling to the edges of tables and shift in your seat as you try not to pass out as another wave of panic crashes through you. you will vomit on your shoes.

you will not be allowed to go home.

you will learn that retreat is safer than attack. that home is safer than outside. that people are cruel for the sake of being cruel and the scars of their words will etch into your brain. you will scratch at your skin and pick at the scabs and mark yourself in the most base animal way of blood and torn flesh. you will make deals with the devil.

you will cry hot tears and smudge your eyeliner. you will wash the streaks off with cold water and be sent back to class. your legs will fold and you will forget how to stand. you will believe them when they tell you that you are doing this on purpose. you will learn to hate yourself the same way they hate you.

you will take tablets designed to sedate and you will still not BE sedate. you will fondle the silver of the blister packs and thank every god you can think of for these small blue marvels that allow you a space to think and be without the constant gnaw of anxiety. you will leave the house and the world won't end. you will learn that these tablets are the only thing that can save you.

you will learn that the people designed to help you don't care whether you live or die. you will learn that being suicidal means a four week wait for an appointment. you will learn about forged care plans and missing medical records. you will listen as medical health professionals lie through their teeth about you. you will wonder why nobody ever took a step back and actually looked at you.

you will stop looking in the mirror. you will feed the hatred and disgust and loathing that grows black and malignant inside of you. you will line up for the firing line and stand, back straight, facing the muzzles of guns because you believe you deserve it. you will think you are a burden. you will be told over and over by charities that say they want to help that you are better off dead. you will hear about the murders of other people like you and hear the sympathy poured out to the murderers. you will learn that your life has less value than normal people.

but—

you will live in spite of it all. you will read and write and draw and paint and create and sing and dance and laugh and love. you will be magnificent. you will feel the catch in your breathing as you walk towards the best day of your life and you will keep walking. you will hold close to you the people who didn't abandon you. you will never, ever be able to give enough thanks to the heroes who ran up the phone bill, who made appointments, who begged and pleaded on your behalf. you will look into your mother's eyes and know that she loves you without conditions. you will live to see your sister's children grow from helpless to incredible. you will sleep with your cat's fur brushing the end of your nose and smile to yourself as she purrs. you will push yourself further than you thought you could survive, and you will survive.

you will survive.
you will survive.

see, here's the secret. to break concrete with your bare hands, you have to train for years, breaking your fingers and healing those fractures until your bones are stronger than your obstacle. every time you've cried, every time someone else's words have broken you, every time you've wished you were dead but survived the night, you have broken and healed the micro-fractures of your soul. you are carbon, turning slowly to diamond. and every single time you were knocked down, you stood back up.

carl sagan once said that we are all made of star stuff. that when the universe first exploded out on itself it created the atoms that eventually became us. so, when your breathing hitches, remember that you are swallowing ancient planets, that every single second since the birth of our reality has been leading up to this moment. so, you're allowed to be afraid.

there's no bravery without fear, no courage without that awful lump at the back of your throat and the turning of your stomach.

you will survive.

because it's been thirteen point seven seven two billion years since you were created, and you are fucking cosmic. you have shone in night skies before day and night existed. you are a fluke, a chance, something so utterly unlikely that the odds are incalculable. and yet there you stand. a miracle.

they'll never understand, the ordinary folk. because they take what they see for granted, and it's not their fault, it's just all they've ever known. you have had to fight for your existence every step of the way. so you know, you know the cost of survival.

and i know, and you can trust me on this, that you are going to claw your way through this life and one day, a long time from now, greet death with a smirk and a firm handshake, utterly unafraid, because fear is something you know, but, like a wolf showing its fangs, your fear makes you powerful.

and i think, maybe, that's why they were afraid of you. because they knew your potential. they knew that you were more. that in the light of the moon you were beautiful. so they tried to hide it from you. tried to beat it out of you.

they failed.

you will survive.

Foreword

19 January 2019

Autistic people really don't like change. I think that's a fair, if broad, statement to make. And yet so much has changed for me in such a short amount of time that I am beginning to question it. I think maybe it could do with some tweaking. Perhaps autistic people don't like change when it is thrust upon them against their will.

When I made my video, 'How To Be Autistic', I made it on a whim, sent it off, and genuinely forgot about it. A year later, it changed my life. And then, I wrote this book. It would be easy to say this is a happily-ever-after story, but I don't want to be disingenuous. Do I still struggle with the same problems I describe at the start of the book? Yes, I still struggle hugely with going out, and I'm still socially isolated. The dark days when the depression causes a near physical ache still happen, more frequently than I'd like. That doesn't just stop because you've been on Sky News, unfortunately. But—I've been given the opportunity to do and experience amazing things. I've felt bolder within myself. I saw Hozier in London, at the venue KOKO, sitting up on the balcony, listening to him sing my favourite song, 'Arsonist's Lullabye'. It was magical, and terrifying, and I don't think I could have done that without the knowledge that I am worth something, that people have judged me and found me not lacking, but inspiring. I went to America! My god, I went to America! I got on my first ever aeroplane and flew above the clouds and landed in New York and hated pretty much every second of it because I'm pretty sure travel is autistic hell—jetlag, food problems, people everywhere, waiting around, new places, new faces, being away from my mum—but I did it. I met Captain America himself at ACE comic con in Chicago (it was only a short hop away and coincided) and even though I look half-dead in the photo and can remember none of the experience, I did it.

Truth is, there are a lot of 'I did it' moments, but they get drowned out by the 'I didn't do it' moments. Humans are bias machines, and we are especially influenced by negatives. We want to believe the worst about ourselves and will pick those scraps up throughout the day and piece them together until we have something that we can look at and say, 'look, aren't I terrible', even if everyone else says otherwise. Maybe that's just me.

To be honest, this whole thing feels like a scam. I keep waiting for the email that says, hang on a minute, you're not a real writer! You don't deserve that art prize! You didn't even finish high school! How dare you! I feel like I've tricked everyone into believing I'm worthy somehow, when really, I don't have a clue. I'm not a grown-up—get someone who knows what they're doing! I follow other autistic people online and they seem to write and indeed suffer, more beautifully, more eloquently, advocate more strongly, and I just sit there, thinking, I don't know what you want me to say.

Then, last night, as I was thinking about how I should write this introduction, it hit me.

When I wrote this book in the fevered rush, on the high of winning and full of hope, yet to come down from it, I knew what I wanted to say, because it was what I'd wanted to say for years. It poured out of me, this burst of words, anger, sadness, hope, joy, trauma. And now, as I reread it, I realise I don't need to compare myself to other people, to how other people perform their autism. If this book helps one person, then it will have been enough. If it inspires one person, it will have been enough.

I hope you're going to wonder why I wasn't diagnosed earlier. It would be easy to dismiss it as 'just how it was back then', but that isn't true. While more people are being diagnosed nowadays, anyone who does not fit stereotypical patterns of autism (male, white, young, straight, cisgender, antagonistic, otherwise mentally healthy, for example) will be passed over. As mental health funding is cut, we face real challenges in getting diagnosed. I talk about my own diagnosis later on, so I won't dwell on it here, but please, if you do feel you or someone you know is autistic, chase that diagnosis and don't give up until you have it. Don't give up after you have it either. Autism, unfortunately, is a life of never giving up. My mum never gave up on me. She could have. Reading this, you would forgive her for doing so. But she never did.

She told me I could be anything. I always wanted to be a writer.

Hey, look, mum, I made it.

I do

22 December 2016

It's 5am on the morning of my little sister's wedding and I've been awake for fifteen hours. I'm tired enough to drop, but sleep evades me. Instead I'm browsing the internet, talking to someone on Twitter, and, oh, I'm all dressed up in a gold velvet-look dress, with curled hair and painstakingly applied makeup.

I'm not going to the wedding—I've told my sister that. She's known for weeks. I don't leave the house, it's just not an option. In the back of my mind I'm thinking maybe I could Photoshop myself into some of the wedding photos, and the thought makes me want to cry.

I'm not going to go. I can't. Even though it's as low key as a wedding can be, at Norwich Castle with maybe a dozen guests, every bit of me resists.

Except.

There's this tiny part of me, often buried, that screams that I need to go. That I need to see my sister get married. The same part of me that nearly cried when I saw her try on her wedding dress for the first time.

4

I do

I look at the webcam photos I've taken of myself. I check the battery and lens of my camera. She wanted me to be the wedding photographer—I was going to be. Until my anxiety decided I couldn't be. My uncle's going to do it instead. He knows what buttons to press.

And I take a diazepam tablet.

Within half an hour I'm wide awake. That's what diazepam does to me—it's called a paradoxical drug effect and it's common in autistic people. It's the same reason coffee makes me drowsy.

The diazepam also calms my mind enough to allow me to think. It's nearly 7am by now and I know my mum will be awake. I send her a message. It's simple, but terrifying for me: *I'm going to Rosie's wedding.*

I try to choke down some food, but the anxiety is clenching my guts and the last thing I want is to throw up or cause a scene. Instead, I wait until I can talk to my mum.

She's pleased—but busy. The wedding is at 10am and Norwich is an hour away. She has to get over to Rosie's to help get Rosie and the kids ready.

I'm back to waiting, and the gremlins are creeping in again.

But I'm going to do this. I have to.

I go over to Rosie's with my dad, and though I don't know it at the time, my mum tells me later that Rosie is thrilled to see me there. Ethan, my nephew, looks dapper in a bowler hat and suit—he's the ring bearer. Ella, my niece, looks gorgeous in a red dress. She's the solitary bridesmaid. The bouquets are handmade with love and care. I grip my camera tighter and take in the scene. This is really happening.

I get in the car, sandwiched between Ethan and Ella in the backseat and I distract myself by chattering nonsense to the pair of them. It's normally a long drive, but today it doesn't feel like it at all. Before I know it, we're parking up near the castle.

When we get out of the car, we discover that Rosie's veil is sitting on the kitchen counter at home, so my brother, Joe, makes a mad dash across Norwich to buy another one. It's a gentle kind of hectic and the wind is heavy and chilly. My sister chose to have a December wedding because she adores Christmas. There will be a Christmas tree at the reception.

We're allowed inside and the waiting begins again in earnest. Anyone with anxiety will tell you that waiting is the worst part of anything. I fill the time by taking candid photos of everyone. Rosie looks beautiful, utterly radiant and everyone else looks so smart. I'm wearing a leather jacket.

Finally, it's time to go in. As I'm the official wedding photographer (my uncle had been fully briefed on the use of the camera, but the role is now mine again) I get to position myself by the window out of the way and watch as everyone gets ready. Nat, Rosie's fiancé, a gentle giant of a man, who rides a motorcycle and is covered in tattoos, and is a thoroughly decent bloke, stands at the front of the room waiting.

And then the music starts up, and my sister walks in, arm in arm with my dad. I start snapping photos, the beep of my camera going off with each one.

The ceremony isn't like what you see on television—it's more intimate, it's weighted and sincere. Rings are exchanged and vows are made and after the kiss I snap a photo of Rosie hugging her new husband, her hand resting on the back of his neck, displaying her new ring, her new commitment. It's my favourite photo of the day.

The official business of signing documents begins and

for whatever reason you're not allowed to photograph that. But they provide dummy documents for the newlyweds to pretend to sign, so I snap more photos. Light filters through the window and makes everything seem ethereal. I just know that these photos are going to be beautiful.

Finally, we file outside and I take photos of the two families that have become one. I'm exhausted, and it shows later in the photos of me, but I'm not Photoshopped in, I'm actually there.

I don't go to the reception. Instead, I go home to sleep.

But my mum tells me that me being there, at the wedding, meant so much to my sister.

And it meant so much to me too.

And looking back, I think that was the first time I beat this thing, the first time I really pushed myself. I got to see my sister get married and I wouldn't change those memories for the world. Anxiety is a huge part of my autism, but for the first time it wasn't in control.

I was.

The 'A' word

I know, I said it, the 'A' word. Autism is a bitter pill to swallow, whichever way you look at it. It's been portrayed as a monster waiting to take your children away from you, it's something isolating, otherworldly, alien and scary. We don't know where it comes from. It just is. And it's all-consuming.

I am autistic in my entirety. There is no part of me that isn't autistic, and that's how I was born. There are correlative reasons as to why this could be—an older father, being a breech baby, being a C-section baby, being two weeks premature, receiving antibiotics after birth, but I don't think it was any of these. I think it's the roll of the dice that genetics gives us. I was born autistic. I will most likely, barring a miracle, die autistic. My brain works differently to neurotypical people's—and theirs in turn work differently to mine.

The best way to describe it is to imagine a road trip. If a neurotypical person wants to get from A to B, then they will most often find their way unobstructed, without road works or diversions. An autistic person will find that they are having to use back roads and cut across fields and explore places neurotypicals would never even imagine visiting, couldn't imagine visiting. A trip from A to B for a neurotypical is a trip through the entire alphabet for an autistic person, at random.

Before you say, 'oh, well, how on earth do you function, if you're having to go all around the houses just to *think*?' remember that the human brain is enormously resilient and builds new pathways where those diversions and road works are. In the same way I can't imagine being neurotypical, you could never conceive of being me. Our brains are sending sparks in different directions and sometimes they end up in the wrong place, but sometimes they end up in incredible places.

I'm not saying that this is a perfect solution. Evolution has not granted us that gift. We still end up in a lot of cul-de-sacs and at a lot of dead ends. But to end this slightly tortured metaphor, I just wanted to say this: if you're neurotypical and reading this, you will never understand what it is like to think like an autistic person.

Unfortunately, it also means we have no idea how you work.

The world is built for neurotypicals; it accommodates you with its loud noises and uncertainty. You're used to it; you don't even have to think about it. You can just pop out without making arrangements weeks in advance, without taking medication, without taking someone with you in case you have a panic attack. You have it so damn easy.

You take what you know for granted, I know, and that's fair enough. It's the brain you were born with. It's just—*frustrating*—for want of a better word, to see you move around this world so easily, while we struggle every day just to be perceived as 'normal'.

Autism has been made into a kind of dirty word. With the help of programmes such as *The A Word* and *The Undateables*, autism is presented as something completely incomprehensible and scary. It's scary because you don't understand it. I get that, it's the same reason I cry when faced with a maths puzzle. I just don't *get it*.

Hopefully though, I can help unravel a few of those mysteries for you, or at least, give you an insight into my life and what it has meant for me to be autistic. It's not necessarily a fun ride, but I promise there's a happy ending. There will be parts that will make you want to cover your eyes or cringe away, but as the person who lived through them, I beg you to read on, because if I can change just one person's perceptions, if I can help one person with autism feel like they're less alone, then this will all be worth it. So please, turn the page. Our worlds are about to collide.

Heavily medicated

Mid 1990s

I was eight years old when I was first prescribed diazepam. There were a multitude of reasons, many of which I'll go on to describe, but at the end of the day, the ultimate reason was that medication is cheaper than doctors, cheaper than psychiatrists, cheaper than psychologists. It's a problem that continues to this day, more so if anything, with drugs being thrown at problems that could be solved if only there were the resources out there to deal with them. Unfortunately, there just aren't.

So, drugs it is then.

As someone who can't really recall ever not being medicated, it's normal for me to reel off a list of medications I've tried and their side effects. Hey, I often even forget a few. So instead I'll just tell you what's working for me right now.

I take two clonazepam (a benzodiazepine) tablets in the morning. I take the equivalent of two trifluoperazine (an anti-psychotic) tablets in the morning. And I take diazepam (another benzo) as needed.

As needed means, essentially, every time I want to leave

the house. Yes, even to visit my sister who lives fifteen minutes away.

I'm reliably informed that there are treatments that could cure me of this, free me of the shackles of medication. That sounds nice. Unfortunately, as I mentioned above, the resources just aren't there. Instead there are waiting lists and locums and handy brochures in waiting rooms. There are private therapists, to be sure, but not everybody can afford that. If you're living below the poverty line, you probably can't afford £50 a week to see a therapist so that you can leave the house comfortably, or make eye contact, or learn vital social interaction skills. So instead you take your meds and, like a crutch, you lean on them, knowing that yes, the benzos are probably messing up your liver, and yes, you should only have been on the anti-psychotics for six months and instead it's been nearly a decade, but what can you do? It works for you. It gives you some semblance of a life. It's incredibly difficult to break that cycle, and if you know how, then please get in touch, because I would love to.

So autistic children are prescribed drugs with side effects they're not told about or able to comprehend. I'm not going to name any names here, but I know of one nine-year-old who has been prescribed citalopram, an SSRI (selective serotonin reuptake inhibitor), which works with anxiety and depression. It's a nasty little drug, one I've taken myself in the past, but the worst part is the withdrawal which, even when done incredibly slowly, can be debilitating.

I don't know if you've ever experienced a brain zap, but it's one of the main side effects of withdrawing from citalopram. It's a brief but horrific experience that throws you completely off kilter. It's like being electrocuted from the inside of your own head. And these brain zaps can last for months, or even longer, after you stop taking the drug.

I wasn't told about this when I was prescribed citalopram at the age of sixteen. When I started to withdraw, I found myself literally unable to walk. The brain zaps though—I wouldn't wish them on anybody.

So, this is what doctors are prescribing to young children. On the one hand, they work. But on the other hand, they're a temporary measure, meaning withdrawal, or worse, they become permanent. Either way isn't great. I mean, I was prescribed diazepam twenty-one years ago, and I'm still reliant on it. There has to be a better way.

My brother and sister are both in medicine; my brother is a junior doctor, and my sister is training to be a nurse. Neither of them received more than a few days training in autism care or diagnosis. My brother trained for five years, he is in charge of people's lives, every day, but the only reason he could ever spot an autistic person who hasn't been diagnosed is because he has lived with one for his whole life.

We talk about awareness. Autism awareness. It gets an entire month. But we're already aware of autism. Everyone knows it exists, thanks to the MMR (measles, mumps and rubella) farce way back when. What we need beyond awareness is action, training, resources.

There's a test you can take to see if you're autistic. It'll take you around ten minutes and it's multiple choice. It's very simple. Just Google 'autism quotient test' and go take it now. I'll wait. The results may surprise you.

Now, this test is not a sure-fire diagnostic tool, but it's definitely a tool that could be used as a stepping stone to further investigation. Think about how easy it was to find online. Think about how easy it would be for a doctor to administer. So why aren't they? Why didn't they when I was a kid?

I wasn't diagnosed until I was twenty-one, you see. And yes, I'm damn well bitter about that. We'll talk about that later. But the first step of my eventual diagnosis was that test. And guess what? I fell perfectly into the category for autism.

It's incredibly frustrating to see that we have this at our disposal and it isn't used as a matter of course. It could make a huge difference and help speed up the process of diagnosis dramatically. As a child, and I quote from my medical records, I went 'from pillar to post' and they still didn't spot it. I don't have enough fingers and toes to count how many psychiatrists and psychologists I'd seen before I'd turned eighteen. Nobody stopped and thought—*hang on here, we've got this ten-minute test at our disposal, let's maybe at least rule out autism as a possibility.*

Something needs to give, something needs to change. We're handing out medication that is unnecessary and/or damaging, we're letting people slip through the net, and we don't have the resources to deal with the fallout.

Prevention is easier than cure. And while there is no cure for autism, there are definitely ways of managing it without the excessive use of medication.

milk teeth

you pulled out our milk teeth
and then you were surprised when we grew fangs in their place

The tooth fairy

Mid 1990s

It started with a wobbly tooth.

The second that tooth wobbled, I stopped brushing my teeth. Eventually, that tooth was knocked out by a dentist in a matter of seconds, but the damage had been done.

I find teeth incredibly disturbing. Even today, the sight or discussion of teeth or dental procedures triggers a panic attack. Only the other day we were watching a programme about vets on the television when they started talking about the dog's dental hygiene. My hands went over my ears and eyes in an instant, and a few seconds later, my mum had muted the television and was keeping an eye out to let me know when it was 'safe'.

I don't know if you know this, but not brushing your teeth is a really, really bad idea. It escalates incredibly quickly and before long you have a rather nasty plaque build-up. Mine got to the point where my bottom lip protruded dramatically from my face, there was at least a centimetre of tartar on my bottom teeth. I refused to go to the dentist. Those wobbly teeth weren't going anywhere, but at a great cost.

The tooth fairy

Why did wobbly teeth freak me out so much? I still don't know. Autistic people are extremely sensitive to sensation, to change, to pain. It could have been any of those things. I don't remember why it made logical sense to stop brushing my teeth, why it freaked me out so much and why it still does, but there we were. I went through the entirety of first school and half of middle school with a mouth full of disgusting, stinking plaque. I learnt to talk around it, and even today when I smile or talk I cover my bottom teeth, even though they're fine now.

It got to the point where my mum arranged to have me knocked out and have all my baby teeth removed and the plaque cleaned off. It was a massive procedure, and it shouldn't have been necessary. The dentist took out eight baby teeth that day, and I was left with gaps and the instruction to gargle warm salt water, which, if you've never tried it, is disgusting.

It took me years to get on top of my dental hygiene. I see a special dentist every three months (in fact, right now I'm overdue for an appointment) and one of the main reasons I was prescribed diazepam was to make it possible for me to go to the dentist. As an adult I've received gas and air to calm me down for a check-up and clean, but I've finally gotten brave enough to go without that. Instead, we have rules:

1) No use of the pick at any stage.
2) Any cleaning must take place in five second intervals, counted out loud by the dentist or hygienist.
3) Nothing more than necessary.

I am proud to say that despite all the trouble I went through with my teeth as a child, I've never had a filling, and the only teeth I've had removed since my baby teeth were my wisdom teeth because they weren't coming through right. I had a general anaesthetic for that, but that's not unusual. I even had stitches, which, as a foreign body in my mouth, should have freaked me out, but I guess because of the positioning so far back, I couldn't really focus on them too much.

I took the stitches out myself. I couldn't face going back to the dentist.

Not cured yet, then.

Procrastination nation

Sorry, I didn't see you there, I was doing literally anything else to avoid writing.

Well, no, that's not quite right. There's a difference between procrastination and executive dysfunction, and I was struggling with the latter. You might not have heard of it before, but it's a rather nasty brain glitch autistic people can have and, if you are autistic, it will probably, at some point, have gotten you yelled at by your parents to *clean your damn room.*

Executive dysfunction is the clear knowledge that a task needs to be completed, but also the clear knowledge that now is not the time to do it.

Trust me, it does make sense.

From fun things like eating or watching a movie or television show, to boring things like washing up or tidying, executive dysfunction sets out the rules of when these tasks can be achieved, and there's very little that can be done to fight it short of being forced into the action.

I need to do the thing, I need to do the thing, I need to do the thing, your brain will repeat. *But not now, but not now, but not now. It's not the right time now. I'll tell you when it's the right time, but it's not now.*

It's incredibly frustrating and indeed upsetting to live with as you see your room becoming messier and messier, the washing stacking up, and you just look at it and—can't.

Imagine you're cosy in bed. You don't have to get up, there's nothing urgent you need to do. But then you realise you're absolutely bursting for a wee. You'll put it off for as long as you can, but eventually you're going to be left with one of two options, and one of them ain't going to be pretty.

With executive dysfunction, your brain forces you to pick the less pretty option, leaving you depressed because you're living in a mess, and everyone else quietly resentful because it seems like the easiest thing in the world to just *pick that piece of paper up off the floor, you've walked past it a dozen times today. Why don't you just pick it up?*

Because it's not for now! Because right now picking up that piece of paper seems the hardest thing in the world and I can't explain it but forcing myself to do it seems utterly beyond any sense of power or control I have. And I know it doesn't make sense, but that piece of paper is going to live there until some arbitrary time when my brain decides that it must be picked up urgently, at once, without fail, at which point the paper will be picked up, but a million other small things will have crept up on me.

And so it goes.

I was always told off as a child for having an extremely messy bedroom. It wasn't for lack of trying, and I didn't realise at the time why it was so hard for me to just pick up clothes or tidy stuff away. But the fact that my brain literally couldn't get its own head around the task meant that I was at an impasse. I couldn't do it until my brain told me to.

And, sometimes, my brain is a little bit useless.

Of course, there are benefits to this—when the arbitrary deadline does arrive it can result in a day-long cleaning spree with bin bags flying and dishes being washed and floors being hoovered. But it's often a long time coming.

Neurotypicals clean in a constant, perpetual manner, whipping out the hoover when there's dog hair on the rug, for example. For me? It's a hell of a lot trickier than that, and for the life of me that's one brain quirk I'll never understand.

Primary school blues

The first time I realised that maybe I wasn't fitting in was in primary school. I went to a very small village school and had a group of friends I was happy with—I couldn't tell you their names or anything about them now, it being so long ago, but I wonder about them sometimes, where they ended up. Regardless, one day, I approached them, and one of them smirked and told me to 'buzz off'. It doesn't sound like much, but for a six-year-old it's pretty devastating. After that it all started to fall apart, and probably would have continued to do so if I hadn't had to move school due to catchment issues.

Another thing that made me unusual was that I would suck milk from bottles at school, the same way a baby would. Now, I know what you're thinking—that's really freaking weird. But I was six years old and six-year-olds do weird things. It was a comfort thing and my mum would make them for me at the same time she'd make them for my baby brother. It wasn't hurting anybody, it wasn't disruptive, it was just something I did.

Until a dinner lady pointed it out and laughed at me for it. I don't remember exactly what she said, but I went home in tears. I never drank from my bottle again, and I realised for the first time that adults could be mean and vindictive for no reason. I don't know what she got out of it—maybe she just didn't like her job, but I think it was a little harsh to take it out on a six-year-old.

At that school I also began to lose my faith in authority figures. There were three incidents I can recall, though the order is a little fuzzy, so I'll go from least to most severe as my mind perceives them.

The first was that we were all due to have our vaccinations at school. Now, having a needle stuck in you is an unpleasant experience and some students, myself included, would be permitted to go home after receiving the vaccinations, because after something like that you just want your mum. Hell, I still feel like that if I need an injection or blood test. So I had my vaccination, and then they told me I couldn't go home. My mum was there to pick me up, but the teachers tried to insist that I stay at school. My mum managed to get me home, but it was the first time I realised that my mum wasn't in control at school, that teachers could break the rules whenever they liked, could go against agreed promises, and had the power to control me.

The second was during a swimming lesson. The school had a small outdoor swimming pool (full of ladybirds) and one day I slipped and went under the water. The next thing I knew I was lying on the tarmac of the playground, looking up at a circle of faces. There was some discussion as to whether my mum should be called, as, after all, I had just nearly drowned, but in the end it was decided that because it was so close to the end of the school day, it wasn't worth the bother. I later found out they never even told my mum about the incident. I learnt then that school was unsafe, and that even if my life was in danger, I would not be permitted to leave.

The final incident was at my first school disco. Now, this was the mid 1990s, in a very small village hall. It wasn't exactly glamorous, but I dressed up and my mum crimped my hair. I got there and the music thrummed through me, and I felt quite unwell. As the evening progressed, I felt more and more unwell until I was lying on a row of chairs with a friend stroking my hair (a surprisingly sophisticated comforting technique for a six-year-old). Suddenly, I sat up and vomited all down myself and on the floor. It was a rather dramatic gesture, but nobody really seemed to notice. I approached a teacher, vomit all down my dress and in my hip-length hair and told them I'd just been sick. They took me to the toilets and tried to clean me up, but it was pretty hopeless. The village hall didn't have a phone, but the building next door did. The disco still had a couple of hours to go, and I was feeling really very ill at this stage, and just wanted to go home. But nobody went next door to phone my parents. I still remember my dad turning up in the car and asking me how the disco went and me in my vomit-stained dress bursting into tears and telling him I was sick.

I remember how angry my mum was at the school, how she went in and gave them a piece of her mind that I'm sure they didn't forget. It was the first time she had to step in for me in regard to them not letting me go home, and unfortunately, not the last. I was off school for the rest of the week with an infection of some kind. What I learnt from that is that even if you're ill, you won't be allowed to go home.

What I learnt from all three of these experiences was that I wouldn't be allowed to go home.

I wish I could say that here endeth the lesson, but unfortunately it had only just begun, and was only going to get much, much worse as I got older.

battle borne

you can't ask me
to apologise
for empathy –
i refuse to.
whilst i
lost
the battle
the war rages on
and i know that
someday
it will be
the most valuable
of weapons.

A little bit of empathy

There's a common misconception that autistic people feel no empathy. This is incredibly damaging and makes it appear that we are either sociopaths or unfeeling robots (I know certain television shows don't help with that sentiment).

I've been told I cannot possibly be autistic because I love my family. That my love for them shows empathy, and that's incompatible with a diagnosis of autism.

This couldn't be further from the truth.

As an autistic person, we cannot rely on body language or facial expressions the way a neurotypical person would. But we are very in tune with emotions. The problem is an excess, if anything, of empathy. We feel your anger, your pain, your sadness. And then we overload, and don't know how to handle that.

I personally go into 'fix-it mode'. Why are you crying and how can I make you stop crying? Who made you angry and how can I make it so you're not angry anymore?

I find myself very sensitive to extremes of emotion and will often mirror them back on the person displaying them, sometimes creating very volatile situations as we bounce off each other.

I really do believe that people don't understand that just because we freeze up around emotion doesn't mean we don't feel it, or know that you're suffering. We just don't know what to do with that information. Which can be tricky.

Sometimes we'll go overboard, like I mentioned, with the fix-it approach. I've come to realise that sometimes people just want someone to listen, not to immediately leap into action. But the urge is still there, the desire to stop the person I love from being in pain.

So no, we are not unfeeling monsters. We feel just as much, if not more, than you do.

It's just that our brains find it hard to deal with that. Autistic people are overloaded by so much, all the time, and this is also true of emotions.

So next time you're upset and an autistic person isn't behaving the way you want them to, don't think of them as uncaring. Realise instead that they're trying to figure out how best to make you feel better, as quickly as possible.

The beginning

Late 1990s

I've been putting off writing this chapter. I stopped writing last night and knew I'd need a run-up. You see, from this point onwards in my life, things started to get very bad very quickly, and it still upsets me a lot to think about it. There are certain people's names I still can't even allow myself to *think*, let alone say aloud, and I still get flashbacks and nightmares of certain memories. I'm going to try to keep it light for you, but it's difficult when I know what lies ahead and what I have to write about. I really, really don't want to write this, but I'm going to, because there might be someone out there who recognises themselves or someone they know in my words. Maybe this'll be cathartic. Here's hoping.

When I was in year two of primary school, we moved to Gorleston and I started at Cliff Park First School. I'm told that when we had looked at schools I'd liked Cliff Park the best of the ones we'd seen. I often wonder if I'd made a different decision all those years ago whether I might be a different person today.

It's hard to join a class when the school year has already

started, but I found people to bond with and made friends fairly quickly, though that meant interrupting existing friendship groups, which was a bone of contention for years afterwards. For a few months everything seemed okay, until I started to feel sick at school.

This was the first time, though I didn't know it then, that I suffered with anxiety about going out. I was seven years old, a prodigious reader, I'd read the Farthing Wood books and the Famous Five books and loved to write and create worlds and stories. I was doing well in all my classes, and nothing seemed out of the ordinary.

But I started to feel sick, every day.

I would tell my teacher, and she would brush it off. Children, I know now, feel sick all the time for various reasons. I know my niece and nephew will sometimes say they feel sick but if you mention you have ice cream, they'll miraculously recover. So I understand why it wasn't taken seriously. But it was the way I reacted to it that I feel should have rung some alarm bells.

I started tilting my head to one side, cricking my neck, in an attempt to ward off the sickness. I don't know why I did this, only that in my mind I thought it would help. I walked around like that, head crooked to one side, feeling desperately ill for the rest of the year. I feel at that point someone should have flagged it up as unusual, because kids don't normally commit to an 'act, or attempt at attention seeking' for that length of time. I don't know—it's difficult to say.

Another oddity I picked up during this time was the absolute refusal to eat my packed lunch at school. It wasn't because I didn't like the food (I'll be discussing food in a later chapter)—I just couldn't eat with the other pupils and refused to do so. It got to the point where the dinner ladies had to monitor me, and would get quite cross with me, watching me as I picked through my sandwiches. Finally, my mum had to be called and I even spoke to her on the phone once as she tried to persuade me to eat.

My problems with my teeth were also beginning around this time. They hadn't become a major issue yet but were bubbling beneath the surface. All the players on the board were lining up—the anxiety, the sickness, the teachers turning a blind eye, and the overreaction to normal milestones.

It was in year three that my world began the holding pattern that would keep me in its clutches for the rest of my school, and indeed, college, career.

When I started year three I was nervous but I had friends and a reasonably okay teacher. For the first term there was nothing unusual, nothing to mention, really. But the day I went back after the first half term, I felt very, very sick. I was sitting in assembly and suddenly, the inevitable happened. I vomited (I think onto someone too, I never found out who, so I owe somebody out there somewhere an apology).

I don't remember the clean-up or even getting out of the assembly hall. I just remember my mum arriving with a tooth-brush. I must have been put into spare clothes at some point. It scares me how little I remember about this first incident, but I do remember my mum turning up. She handed me my toothbrush and I didn't want to brush my teeth because the sinks were in full view of the rest of the class and I'd already embarrassed myself enough. I asked if I could go home.

My mum said no.

I've never asked her about why she said no. Maybe she knew back then that it wasn't a 'real' illness, or maybe she just thought I'd be okay after getting it out of my system. I desperately wanted to go home—being sick is traumatic and

I thought I was ill. I was too young to realise that my brain and thoughts could make me just as ill as an upset stomach could.

At any rate, I didn't get to go home. I re-joined the class.

Mum, I know you're reading this, and I'm sorry, but it was that day that I realised, *maybe Mum isn't going to come save me either*. As a child, your mum is your everything, and mine in particular because my dad worked all the time so we could afford to live and eat. We were extremely close and still are, but that shook me.

I'm writing this now with a lump in my throat. I don't know why she said I couldn't go home. I'm sure she had her reasons. In the years to come though, I would hear that a lot, too many times to possibly count.

I know now that she was probably trying to do what was best for me. But as a child, how do you deal with the fact that the one person who is supposed to protect you, isn't?

I lost something vital that day, and my anxiety began to devour me. Knowing I couldn't go home, couldn't escape, meant that at first I was throwing up and feeling sick after every half term, but by the time I reached middle school, it was after every weekend. And that's when things started to get farcical.

(Mum, I love you, and I know you'd do anything to protect me. This is a representation of my feelings at the time. I know it will probably upset you to read this, but I don't want to tell anything other than the truth in this book. This is the hardest thing I've ever had to write and we're not even at the bad bit yet. I'm going to come give you a hug now and say sorry. Maybe have a bit of a cry. It's okay, we got out the other side alive, didn't we? It took twenty years to get there, but we did it.)

The middle

Late 1990s

I started middle school with all the issues I had left first school with and with a new one—bullying.

I think a level of strangeness is acceptable when you're a kid, up to a point. Children accept a lot—they don't have the same prejudices as adults, and they're very open-minded. But unfortunately, as we grow, we begin to absorb the opinions of the world around us, and the unusual becomes disquieting and something worthy of mockery.

Someone I had considered a friend began bullying me when I entered year four. We'd been part of the same friendship group in first school, but there had been an unspoken competition about who got to be best friends with another child, and I'd come away with the 'prize', as it were. The girl who had been left to the side started making the odd snide comment and gossiping about me behind my back. Looking back, it wasn't anything too harsh, but isn't it weird how knowing someone is talking about you and not knowing what they're saying is somehow worse than knowing what they're saying upfront?

I had an amazing teacher in year four, she took me under her wing and tried her absolute hardest with me. I'd started walking with a hunch, curling in on myself, and she would keep me in at lunch times and break times and sometimes even after school for a bit, using her time to try to get me to stand up straight. Now, having grown up I understand the concept of victim blaming, and I know she wasn't doing this consciously and I don't blame her for her efforts at all—she honestly was trying to help me. I think of her with great fondness and I really hope she reads this and knows that she was one of the best teachers I ever had, and definitely the most invested in me. Thank you, Mrs C., you were amazing, and I still remember your rule never to use the word 'nice' to describe anything, ever. In fact, year four was the first time I really started to write, and I shone at it. She really encouraged me, and I don't think you'd be reading this now if I hadn't gotten lucky and had her as a teacher.

So, bullying, and walking around like a scared mouse waiting for the fox to pounce: the sickness had escalated, and was now playing to its own whims. I threw up in the middle of class, uttering a small 'sorry' afterwards. I threw up into my teacher's hands (I imagine she's never forgiven me for that, and rightly so, that's just disgusting). I spent more time hunched over a toilet than I did in lessons, it felt like. Another place I made my home was outside of 'The Office', where the secretaries would phone your mum if you were ill. I spent a lot of time there, waiting and hoping to be picked up.

By now, my mum was aware that she couldn't come get me every single time I threw up. But I didn't understand that. I would sit outside the office for hours, watching as other students went home, and wondering what made me different, why I was ill and why nobody was helping. The receptionists were sick to the back teeth of me, and rightly so, it must have been very annoying. But I was looking for an escape route. The bureaucracy of it all went over my head, I was just trying to survive in a world that seemed to be becoming increasingly harsh.

School trips were the worst. They were an instant anxiety trigger and would lead to much vomiting. This was back when parents could go on school trips without needing any special checks, so I was lucky enough that my mum or dad would always volunteer to come along (and what brave souls they were). My dad, bless him, would always fall asleep on the coach, while I fiddled with my anti-travel sickness wristbands and tried to ignore the other kids whose travel sickness was significantly worse than mine.

The last thing to talk about with regards to year four, and I think a lot of autistic people and parents of autistic people will nod along with this, is handwriting. Now, this was back before computers. I wouldn't even type on a computer for two years yet, they were a very new thing, and I know this is hard for any youngsters reading to believe, but there you go. We had to learn to write neatly, because that was the only way you could write—on paper, with a pen. Or in my case, a pencil. My previous school had taught me cursive before printing, so I had one advantage there. The only problem was that my cursive, and indeed my print, was so appallingly bad that I could have qualified as a doctor on the strength of that alone. To graduate from pencil to pen in your workbooks, you had to prove that your handwriting was neat enough. I watched throughout the year as pens were handed out to my classmates. My work was more than once held up as the worst in the class, an example of what not to do.

I never did graduate to a pen. To this day, I'm illegally using biros without the consent of Mrs C. Something about that tickles me tremendously. I was the only one, on the last day of year four, still to be a pencil user. Don't tell the police, I don't want my secret pen usage getting me into trouble.

And yes, my handwriting is still appalling to this day. I can't hold a pen properly, and people always point it out and comment on how strange it is. I'm including this because I know it is one of the things autistic people talk about sometimes. I just want us to have a moment where we nod to each other and say 'yep, that was me'. Or, maybe you did graduate to a pen. If so, what was your secret?

The sick bowl

1999

I left year four doing really well educationally but appallingly socially and mentally. While exams did make me vomit, I also passed them with flying colours. Entering a new class meant moving the seats around, and I was left on my own, without any of my friends. More people were picking up on the bullying trend, including one girl who seemed to make it her mission in life, and who continued right through to the end of high school. I'd love to name her, but I won't. I will talk about her more later, because her final feat was a bit of a doozy. Weirdly, a few years back she tried to add me on Facebook. I must admit, I really don't understand people sometimes.

Now, I've been putting off writing this chapter, because it's going to be both gross and upsetting. I know there's already been so much vomit in this book that you're probably wondering how much one person can vomit. Let's just say, I was really, really skinny. I was very underweight by the time I reached year five. Considering I'd been a rather chunky toddler, this was a very dramatic shift.

Year five was the year the memo went around that I would throw up at the drop of a hat. On the first day of the year the teacher made sure to keep me out of the classroom for most of the day, sending me on errands and keeping me within running reach of the toilets. So began my somewhat unwanted infamy.

Soon though, it became clear that errands and knowing the fastest route to the nearest bathroom weren't enough, and so began the era of The Sick Bowl.

The Sick Bowl was a washing up bowl (you know the sort, every household has one). I would walk into the playground with it clenched under my arm, and I would place it on my desk during class.

You're wondering why nobody thought this was weird. So am I.

As this all builds up, I want to remind you that I hadn't been diagnosed with *anything* at this stage. I'd not been tested for anything, and I wouldn't enter the CAMHS (Child and Adolescent Mental Health Services) system for another year yet. I had been prescribed diazepam, which I was taking without understanding what it was (how do you describe anxiety to a child?).

You might be wondering why we didn't research this ourselves, as a family. As I mentioned previously, this was pre-computers, and pre-internet. The only autistic child my mum had ever met was non-verbal and had a lot of very different difficulties. It never occurred to her that I could possibly be autistic, it wasn't an option. Without that seed of knowledge, how could we possibly research something? We were a family of five, with my younger siblings growing up normal and healthy, and I was a huge energy sink. The headmaster of the school joked that my mum should have her own office within the school because of how often she was up there to talk about me.

I wasn't naughty or disruptive. In fact, despite it all, I was in the top set in all my classes, and when I did speak I was eloquent and mature sounding. I was shy, but that's not that unusual. I think it was this that led people to believe that my symptoms were either a) made up to get attention or b) just a phase. Walking into school with the knowledge that I was going to be sick, that all the teachers, the headmaster and the receptionists knew this was a certainty, that I was withdrawing into myself and had difficulties with friendships, were all signs that should have been picked up by a doctor. And it's hard to comprehend, now, why they weren't.

We saw the doctor a lot. My mum had begun what I think a lot of mothers of children with autism will recognise: the frantic phoning of anyone who could possibly help. She fought for me every day, even though at this time she was extremely unwell herself and had two other children to raise. I put her through so much anguish, and it must have killed her to know that picking me up would probably be the worst thing she could do because then the escape route would have been established and I'd have known that home was only a phone call away. She has told me since how hard it was, and how she was constantly told off about my poor attendance and behaviour. I don't fault her for any of it. She tried so damn hard and has continued to do so. I don't have enough words to thank her for everything she's done and the phone bills she's had to pay. The truth is though, despite the fact that she was practically shouting, nobody was listening.

Entering the digital age

2000

Year six began with another great teacher—Ms M.—who, once again, was supportive of my writing and encouraged me all the way. She had a laminated book of the best stories written by her pupils and I have to admit I ended up in there more than a couple of times. My brother and sister would also find fame by getting their stories in that self-same book. Years later, when I met the teacher again, she referred to it as our family's book.

It was really nice to be praised for my writing, as meanwhile everything else was falling apart. The Sick Bowl was still my constant companion. Once again, my friendship group had been split up and the friends I'd made the previous year had made their own clique and I was left alone.

Another girl started to bully me quite intensely, along with the girl I previously mentioned. I dreaded going to school and would often cry after getting home from particularly bad days. My mum would wake me up every morning and I would lie in bed praying she'd forget somehow, that I could just stay home. Stay safe.

There was one saving grace to year six though, and that was that the classroom had a computer. It didn't have internet or anything as fancy as that: this was back in the dial-up days when you paid by the minute and our school definitely couldn't stretch to that. But it did have a word processor. It was hard to wrangle time on the computer, but I took to it instantly. It was the first time I realised I had a natural affinity for technology.

At home, too, we got a computer that year. I know it cost an extortionate amount, the sort of price you'd pay for a high-spec gaming computer these days, but it had an encyclopaedia, a few children's games, and if I remember correctly, a motorcycle racing game none of us could play without crashing within the first lap. It also had a word processor, and a few months later, a dial-up router.

The ping-bzzt-ting of dial-up is forever burnt into the memories of many, and I loved it. We paid by the minute and had a monthly limit of sixty minutes, but it was a portal into an entirely new world. I used it to read and explore and learn. It sparked an interest in graphic design and website building, and so I started to teach myself HTML and CSS coding.

Back in the day there were no website builders like there are now—everything had to be hand coded, usually in Notepad, and uploaded very, very slowly through your dial-up service. If I say the words 'Geocities' or 'Angelfire' to kids nowadays they have no idea what I mean, but back then, they meant everything to me. I could write and publish that writing in a matter of minutes (well, relatively speaking), I could find other people's writing, and share links and socialise without being face to face. I joined Neopets and, as it was essential that your pet's page looked good, learning

HTML and graphic design became a must.

Expressing myself online became second nature, and while I always had a habit of oversharing, it meant I was able to talk about things I couldn't talk about to anybody else. Even though I was shouting into the void (these were the days of Ask Jeeves, after all, so search engine optimization terms weren't exactly a thing) it felt meaningful. It sparked a love affair with the internet that I have never lost. For better or worse, I'd found a sanctuary, a home. The internet helped me feel less alone.

It was around this time that I began isolating myself from the world outside and stopped going out with my family. I know my mum has told me she tied herself up in knots about it. On the one hand, she was leaving me at home on my own, but on the other, I was much happier there. If she'd taken me out I would have been miserable and dragged the day down.

Isolation is a big part of autism, and I will talk about it more later, but that was when it really began for me. I didn't hang out with friends, and when family members or family friends came round I would go to my room—the only people I saw were my mum, my dad, Rosie and Joe. This would be echoed in my later life during my twenties, and I'm certain this was the beginning of my agoraphobia.

Another quirk I picked up during this time was refusing to eat dinner with my family. We used to have family meals and my mum loved to have everyone sit and chat and just enjoy one another's company. One night after a day of playing in the garden, I was sat at the table when I felt a sharp stabbing pain in my stomach. I'd never felt anything like it, and I made to get up so I could go through to the kitchen to tell my mum, but I never made it that far.

The next thing I knew I was in a racing car driving across the desert, my heart beating too fast.

Then I had fallen out of bed.

After that, I could hear voices and it was dark. They were telling me to be calm and try to get out from under the table. I'd had a fit and collapsed. My mum was panicked, and I was really shaken. I went to the hospital and was checked out and pronounced fine. Brain scans later showed nothing was wrong, and the doctor told me 'everyone is entitled to one unexplained fit'. But the experience stuck with me, and for fear of it repeating, I stopped eating meals with my family. I still don't to this day. I've only just gotten to the point where I can eat basic food stuffs in front of other people. For some reason it feels safer to eat on my own, so that even if it did happen again, nobody would see it and it wouldn't be so bad.

The fear is still there and still very real.

Autism logic, you just can't beat it.

Speaking of food

My diet is very limited. It always has been. I've been called many things—a picky eater, anorexic—but the truth is it's an Autism Thing.

A lot of autistic people struggle with different tastes and textures. Routine is also very important and knowing what you're going to have for dinner and how long it's going to take is very reassuring. Having a limited, same-thing-every-day kind of diet gives that reassurance.

It is, however, really, really boring.

I don't know why I'm so reluctant to try new foods. I think I have some kind of sixth sense for whether I'll like something or not, and the answer is nearly always 'not'. It doesn't help that I'm vegetarian and most vegetarian food includes, well, vegetables. My go-to joke about being a vegetarian who doesn't really eat fruit or vegetables is that I laugh in the face of scurvy, but I feel that maybe the scurvy will be laughing in the long run.

A typical day for me food-wise goes like this:

Breakfast: A Wispa bar and a glass of milk.

Lunch: Toast (but it has to be the Tesco Stay Fresh brand and it has to be toasted for exactly the right amount of time and I have to eat it within a certain time frame or I can't eat it). Sometimes I'll have two rounds, sometimes I'll have four.

Dinner: Quorn Lasagne.

Sometimes, if I'm feeling particularly flush with my money, I'll order a Chinese, but the order is always the same—Mushroom Chow Mein. And then I pick the mushrooms out, because while I like them for the flavour they add, they're what I imagine eating slugs must be like.

As a result, I've always been very thin, and I probably don't get enough calories. I don't really count them. There is hope though, after years of being six stone and chronically underweight, my metabolism has finally given up the ghost and I gained a stone in a year. Weirdly though, when I saw my scoliosis surgeon and he looked at my x-rays, he did comment about how we needed to talk about my weight loss, which was confusing because I'd gained weight and actually weighed the most I'd weighed, well, ever!

It's very, very difficult to introduce new foods into my diet, and I have to do it on my own terms, and with the proviso that nobody is going to comment if I don't like it. I still can't break my daily routine, but if there's cheese and tomato pizza going spare I can eat a slice, or if there's ice cream in the freezer, as long as it's vanilla or vanilla and chocolate, I'll give it a go.

For those looking for answers to similar problems, I really don't know what to suggest. Try finding foods that are similar to what you already like. I know I sometimes go on my preferred supermarket's home delivery site and just spend an hour looking at what's new and what I could potentially try. To a certain degree you just have to go for it and be brave (and have a glass of water on hand in case you don't like it). Don't consider it a failure if you can't handle the texture or taste of something, just mark it down as a 'well, at least I tried it'. You might find something you like.

To parents of autistic kids desperately struggling with meal times, you have my deepest sympathies. The best thing you can do is avoid forcing the issue, it will only garner resentment and fear. Let your child move at their own pace, and if they show an interest in something you're eating (staring as you eat it, or saying it smells nice, for example), maybe offer them a bit. Don't make a big thing of it, just treat it as the most boring, regular thing in the world. If you're worried about them missing out on dietary requirements, look into giving them vitamins. Actually, autistic people out there reading this, take your vitamins! Despite what I said earlier, it would really, really suck to get scurvy. I mean, it would make a great anecdote, but the symptoms are just awful. Get your vitamin C.

I've come a long way with my eating habits one way or another. Textures still really bother me, as do 'bits', like in orange juice, and I'll never be able to eat anything spicy or drink anything fizzy, but I can go to Tesco after looking stuff up online and then in the privacy of my own room tentatively take a taste of a new food.

If you're bored enough, you'll try new things.

Or, if you're like me, and cursed with some very strange bad luck, the supermarket will stop making the thing you've been living off for the past two years and you'll have to find something new. Rest in peace, Tesco's Vegetarian Lasagne, you were a god among foods and your replacement will never compare. I could have cried when they were discontinued. I still miss them to this day. If you could just pause and take a moment's silence for their loss, it would be greatly appreciated. Thank you.

Skank

2001

Year seven opened with a teacher I would not call particularly caring or warm. She liked to make fun of pupils and humiliate people, and on one occasion when I was off school she called the register and made a joke about my surname, which I only found out about because my friends told me. When my mum went up to the school (I was being bullied enough without the teachers joining in), the teacher hotly denied it, and it was only because my friend was standing beside me and backed me up that she admitted what she had done. On more than one occasion she pointed out to the class that I'd messed something up—not cutting something out properly or not colouring something in neatly enough.

Besides her, though, year seven wasn't a bad year. It was my final year of middle school and I sat at a table with three very different people, but as a group we bumbled along and I grew particularly close to one boy, on whom I soon realised I had a crush.

I've since learnt with crushes that I go all-in once I have one—and this was no exception. And I have also found that sometimes, if I'm very lucky, people like me back, and on this occasion, he did. There was the awkward asking out that was probably far more dignified than any Tinder exchange these days, and then, apparently, we were boyfriend and girlfriend.

And my alarm bells started ringing like no tomorrow. I started to avoid him entirely, not speaking to him at all. My anxiety went through the roof and I spent every single day outside the office.

My other friends took it upon themselves to lock us in the bike shed together after school and not let us out until we kissed. Thankfully, after much begging on my part, we were let out without having to.

A few days later we broke up. It had been brief, and terrifying, and we hadn't even held hands, and I still liked him, but I couldn't deal with the 'responsibility', as it were, of a relationship. And yes, I was taking this way too seriously for a year seven relationship, but I do have that habit. I stayed friends with him though, right through high school and into college, where he came out as gay—as did nearly all of my friendship group from around that time. It's true what they say—we travel in packs!

The girl I mentioned earlier who would go on to make it her school career's mission to bully me continued in earnest, hissing insults at me every time she passed me in the corridor. Her favourite was 'skank'. I didn't know what it meant at the time, I just knew that it was hurtful and I couldn't understand why she was targeting me. I still don't—I'd always tried to be nice to her and it didn't make any sense. The only thing I can figure is that she had problems of her own. I would find out in high school that I wasn't the only one she targeted, but it wasn't an excuse. It hurt and I think not knowing why she was doing it made it much worse.

Pokemon cards were all the rage back then, and also very much banned at my school. I had a science teacher I really liked called Mr P. and I asked him nicely if we could start a Pokemon Club, where Pokemon cards would be allowed (one of my friends was lucky enough to have family connections that allowed him to get Japanese cards), and we could watch recorded episodes of the TV show. Pokemon Club went well, until one day I happened to arrive early to see the two boys who were put in charge of guarding the classroom at lunchtime, rifling through my cards, which I had stored for safe keeping in the teacher's desk drawer. My anxiety prevented me from saying or doing anything, but later that lunchtime I found out my shiny Charizard was missing. I knew they'd taken it, and the teacher knew who they were, but because Pokemon cards were banned there was no recourse, nothing we could do. I was absolutely gutted. At the time Charizard was the rarest card around, and, yes, I shouldn't have taken him to school, but I was always very trusting and believed that authority figures would do the right thing and were going to protect me, despite my previous experiences. These illusions would be shattered utterly in high school, but my mum had raised me to be respectful to my elders and so I was. To find out that I had been stolen from and, despite the culprit being obvious, there was nothing to be done, was hard.

The last day of middle school was a happy day. My mum told me that high school would be different, people would be more mature and it would just be better. I would hear that about college too, except with the addition that people would be there to learn rather than taunt.

I took in a disposable camera and took a bunch of photos of people who, looking back now, seem astonishingly young.

I can't believe we were ever that young, but we were. I had an autograph book, which I got everyone in my class to sign—this was before yearbooks were really a thing, so almost everyone had one. My art teacher wrote that I should continue to draw. My year six teacher wrote something lovely too. There was only one really negative comment, surely meant in jest, but it hurt nonetheless, and in hindsight was made in extremely poor judgement: an assistant to a boy I was friends with wrote something along the lines that I should get help with my mental health. I feel that was out of order, because I don't think he meant it in an advisory tone, but rather, as he often pointed out to me, that I was some variation on crazy.

I've since burnt the autograph book, along with my high school yearbook and planner. I still have the photos somewhere, but I don't like to look at them. It feels like looking at Rome before the fall. I was on the precipice of disaster and I didn't even realise it. For all that I was struggling already, it was about to get far worse, and despite what my mum had promised, high school would not be better.

under flickering yellow light

burn it all to
the fucking ground
and start again
with what is left

paint your face
with the ashes
of who you used to be
and bare your teeth
against the dark

when you feel
the snap of bone breaking
under your closed fist
remember they did this to you
smile because they wanted a monster

and you fucking gave them one

blood doesn't look black in the moonlight
it gleams crimson
and there's no shame in looking twice
because it's beautiful to behold

and when you wash it from your knuckles
in the sink
of some all-night gas station
and it turns the water pink

and when you catch a glimpse of yourself
in the mirror under flickering yellow light
invisible scars pulsing under your skin
bite at chapped lips
and try to believe that you recognise the reflection
veteran of a thousand wars
hollowed out daily
until all that remained was some mercenary creature
feral grin and wild eyes
remember that this is how they moulded you
some half-crazed thing
not scared any more

you are a reckoning

High school part I

I don't want to start writing about high school. I really, really don't. This is the hardest thing I will ever have to write about, and my stomach is churning, and I just want to close this document and run away, abandon the entire project. I'm scared. It's been thirteen years since I left and I'm still so freaking scared. I just want to burst into tears. So I'm sorry if this is a little disjointed, a little emotional, and doesn't make sense at times. Of all the things I'm going to talk about here, these chapters are going to be the hardest, and I guess I'm mentally psyching myself up for that now. Okay, here goes.

When I started high school, I'd been in the CAMHS (child and adolescent mental health services) for a few years. I was still vomiting on a regular basis and no amount of talk therapy was helping. I was still on diazepam when needed, and I had seen nobody over the summer. I had spent my time online, in my room. I was sure though, that high school would be better. It had to be, right?

I want to stress that I still had no diagnosis at this stage. I was struggling a lot with eye contact and with my teeth, the response to which was to force me to make eye contact and force me to read a truly horrific book about teeth that I still remember vividly and have flashbacks about. I know it was recommended that I should watch *The Breakfast Club*, a movie I now love, about a group of high school students from different cliques being forced into detention together and finding common ground, but I'm glad I didn't follow that advice, because the knowledge that 'we're all the same underneath' would have been brutal, because it would have meant that these fundamentally good people, pupils and teachers alike, were being cruel when the option was there for them not to be. I struggled a lot with seeing psychiatrists and psychologists, because they didn't seem to understand me. Having seen my medical records, I now know that I was described as having 'an adolescent crisis'—what on earth does that mean?

On the first day of high school, I arrived to find I'd been put in a form with none of my friends. Before I'd joined the school, we'd all been asked to write down three people we'd like to be in a form with. The high school had merged several different schools together and for the first time, not everyone would know everyone else. I made my way up the three flights of stairs to my new form room and found myself surrounded by strangers. I went through that first day in a strange daze, going to lessons and sitting wherever there was a space, just going through the motions.

I got home that evening and after crying with my mum for a while, she told me she would fix it—and she did. The next day I was moved to a new form with one of my best friends from middle school, a girl I knew and would actually go on to hang out with outside of school a few times that year. I often look back at this intervention, and the hand fate dealt me and wonder. The teacher had a reputation for being able to deal with troubled students, the skivers and low achievers and all that. I can't even think her name to myself now without my head filling with white noise. I can't even give you her initial. She is what my nightmares are made of. She is my flashbacks. But at the time, she seemed the kind of woman who wouldn't say boo to a goose, chubby and short and warm, welcoming and deceptively nice. She promised to look after me.

I settled into my new form and lucked out, ending up on a table with an amazing group of people. We bonded quickly and my childhood best friend from primary school sat beside me, the one who had unwittingly caused the rift that led to my first bully. We were a table of six and we found each other in our various classes, forming firm friendships. We worked well as a cohesive group. In pairs we had little in common, but when we were together something sparked and there was that rare sense of belonging, without demand or expectation. It was nice—and I remember one Christmas we all decided to buy presents for each other. It's actually my fondest memory of high school (not that there are many), but it was back when you could go up town with £10 and come home with change, and so with a little money we all bought and wrapped presents and lugged them into school, opening them before the first lesson of the day.

We were loud and rambunctious, revelling in good spirit and new gifts, thanking each other and noticing the jealous glares from the tables around us. The teacher soon stepped in and told us to put it all away immediately. The levity dropped like a stone, but for those few minutes, I felt truly happy and as though I belonged.

I had an amazing, if slightly bizarre, English teacher,

who singled me out as the most talented writer in the class (sadly, in front of the class, which did me no favours whatsoever), and encouraged me greatly. He also made the slightly unwise choice of talking about the Doomsday Clock without context, explaining that we were five minutes away from midnight, from nuclear annihilation. He also showed us the animated film *When The Wind Blows*, the story of an old couple following the government advice and trying to save themselves from a nuclear bomb, only to slowly die from radiation sickness. I went home that evening distraught, sure that at midnight the bomb would fall and I would die.

A lot of parents complained, and the teacher apologised a few days later. He was a weird one, and disappeared to live on a boat off the coast of Australia towards the end of the year.

Academically, I was doing well. I was in top set for all my subjects, and parents' evenings and report cards always had only one complaint—that I should speak up more in class. There was one shadow hanging over me though—my attendance. As it dropped below ninety per cent, my mum was called more and more often, to the point where there was a very real risk that she would get in trouble for not sending me in. So even though I spent every morning hoping she'd forget to wake me, and even though I spent at least one day a week camped outside the office begging to go home, I was stuck at school, throwing up my breakfast and spending my time in class desperately trying not to pass out or dissociate (I'll talk about that more later).

It was decided that my mum would hand over the decision of whether I should go home or not to my form teacher. I was now completely at the mercy of a woman who was in a position of power over me, who didn't know me the way my mum did—and couldn't possibly imagine the damage she'd end up doing to my mental health in the long term.

It was the worst decision my mum could have made, but it was the only one she could have made. I don't blame her for it, though I did at the time. I couldn't understand why she had stopped saving me. She'd always been my 'safe person', and suddenly I couldn't run to her. As I dashed from classrooms to vomit, and shook and lost track of my surroundings in class, it felt like I was on death row, but with no chance of a call from the governor at the last minute. Every day it felt like I was walking those final few yards to the electric chair. I became more and more withdrawn, and all my symptoms increased to a point where they were borderline unmanageable. My mum told me later she looked into home schooling but it just wasn't an option.

I wanted an escape route. I didn't want to carry on. For the first time, I actively wanted to die.

Towards the end of year nine, we were told that the school would be introducing a house system, and rather than having one year group in each form, the four year groups would be mixed together, meaning that everyone would be split up and rearranged. As I sat in that assembly my stomach dropped. I was about to lose the friends I had made, at the point when I needed them most. The teacher pulled me aside afterwards and told me she'd watched my face fall at the news. I don't know why she told me that…maybe she thought it was funny.

Either way, school was about to get even more lonely, and my anxiety was headed for the big leagues.

High school part II

2003–2005

It's in year ten that you start studying for your GCSEs, and I'd chosen subjects based on whether I'd enjoy them or not, without really considering anything beyond the present. I wanted to be an author when I grew up, but really had no solid plans. I assumed college would follow high school, and then university—I had lofty goals of going to Oxford or Cambridge, I'd been exposed to Stephen Fry at an early age, and hearing he'd come from Norfolk and done so well for himself, I believed I could too. I'd already altered my natural Norfolk farmer accent to speak more like him, and yes, he was my idol, the person I knew I would be when I grew up. Successful, living in London, and writing brilliant books.

The subjects I chose beside the mandatory ones were media studies, art, history and textiles. I only chose textiles because a design and technology subject was compulsory. It was taught by the teacher who had already tormented me for two years, and yet I still trusted that she had my best interests at heart. It's hard to explain that, as a child, I was incredibly naïve about a lot of things and very bad at reading people.

When she was cruel I believed she was being kind. When she pointed out my flaws, I strove to correct them. I didn't realise that maybe her cruelty was for the sake of cruelty. I still had my faith in authority figures, because surely, they wouldn't be *allowed* to be authority figures if they were the bad guys, right?

I'd chosen history because the subjects we'd be learning sounded utterly fascinating—history of medicine, the American West, policing during Jack the Ripper's reign of terror, and the Vietnam War. As we started the history of medicine, history quickly became my favourite subject and I became utterly enthralled by all things related to medical history, from the gruesome to the utterly brilliant. I really liked the teacher too, Mr H., was enthusiastic as well as being both bitter and cynical. He didn't suffer fools gladly, but had time for those who put the effort in. Years later I would write a letter to him thanking him for teaching me, and though he never responded, I'd like to think it meant something to him.

I still have a huge passion for the history of medicine, and read about it as much as I can, as well as watching any and all documentaries about it. My search for knowledge has expanded to modern medicine as well and the incredible strides we've made, but my understanding of how primitive medicine used to be and the progress we've made in the last hundred years alone gives me a huge amount of perspective and I am constantly in awe of scientists, doctors and surgeons. My brother is a junior doctor, and I often pump him for as much information as he is allowed to give about what he's seen. He's very careful not to break doctor-patient confidentiality, so I can't get much from him, but he's always a resource for checking out the latest discoveries and trying to weasel out whether they're fact or fiction.

The Vietnam War was another topic that absolutely blew me away. The sheer brutality of it, and of American interventionism, and the guerrilla warfare tactics of the Viet Minh astounded me, and I find I can still apply a lot of what I learnt to politics today.

I also had an amazing English teacher, who was vibrant and seemed excited about the subject. He'd read aloud and do all the voices and challenge us to think outside the box. He pushed me to write more and called me the most modest student in the class, which I didn't really understand at the time, and by mentioning it now, I've kind of ruined it. Meeting him years later after completing a manuscript I had hoped would become a book and asking him to read it, my illusions were shattered. I understood the phrase 'never meet your heroes' fully for the first time (though since then I've met other heroes and they've been awesome, so terms and conditions do apply). He told me how he'd hated being a teacher and how my book would never be published because 'zombies have gone out of fashion' (it was a book about vampires, but okay). I was gutted.

Media studies was another subject I did well in. In fact, I coasted it, making nearly no effort and still getting the highest grade in the class. I made a friend there, a grunge boy who introduced me to Nirvana, and helped me learn more about the music that you just didn't hear on the radio. I'd already been branching out, and having a musician for a dad meant I'd been exposed to far more music growing up than most, but rock music and alternative music were something new and exciting, and these singers were angry, hurt and honest. I'd found my people, and the fact that Kurt Cobain was already long dead broke my heart. I'd listen to his music for hours on end and try to replicate his song writing. I had an electric guitar, but really wasn't good at chords, nor could I read music. Even now I still pick up a guitar from time to time. I love the idea of making music, and writing songs, but my hands are just not made for playing the guitar. My dad is nice enough to let me sing with him on occasion, and it's always a really fun experience. And I get to sing and dance with my niece and nephews without the fear of being judged. But as I was saying before I went off on a tangent, I'd discovered rock music, and it was amazing.

Rock musicians were the first successful tattooed people I saw. My mum had a tattoo, the family's initials on her wrist, but other than that it seemed like a culture I couldn't belong to. The members of one band in particular, Good Charlotte, were covered from head to foot. Something in my brain switched on at that moment, and I started counting down to my eighteenth birthday.

Meanwhile, I was spending more and more time outside the office asking to go home, only to be sent to my form teacher and told I couldn't. I would return to class in tears, and I could tell other teachers had sympathy for me, but there was nothing they could do. There was a hierarchy in place, and they couldn't (or wouldn't) rebel against it. My grades started to slip dramatically, and I couldn't concentrate in class at all. My essays still got high marks, but I did poorly in anything that had to be done during school hours. The tipping point was my mock GCSEs. I was so ill with anxiety the morning of them that I couldn't even go in, but my form teacher phoned my mum and angrily explained that I must, so feeling like death I sat my maths mock, and stared at the questions uncomprehendingly. I'd had a really bad maths teacher for the previous two years, who would disappear off for coffee for half the lesson and who didn't care at all about actually teaching, just leaving us to read from books and trying to solve problems with no knowledge of the techniques required. I answered the first four questions before giving up. I couldn't pass this exam. I spent the rest of the time doodling in the blank spaces and on my desk. The same was true of my statistics, biology and physics exams.

Getting the results back was a real blow not just to me, but probably to my parents as well. My history teacher, who had always been kind to me, pulled me aside and told me I'd gotten a D in the exam, and that there was no way I was going to pass my actual GCSE paper. I was politely asked by the maths department head to withdraw from the statistics exam and give someone else a go, because I'd scored the second lowest in the class. My science teacher, an awful woman, made no effort to mentor me or try to improve my work. She despised me, and I her, she saw me as a slacker and a skiver, and I was afraid of her. I gave up on even trying to learn during her lessons, instead letting the anxiety wash over me and just waiting them out.

My bully, lovely girl that she was, finally escalated things to a point that was no longer ignorable, and in full view of the school receptionists, got her lackey to grab my hands from behind as she yelled abuse in my face. That evening I went home and told my mum, and the girl and her lackey were suspended. From the other people she'd also been bullying I got knowing nods of approval. From people I didn't expect, I got hissed threats and was told I'd made it all up. But when she came back, she didn't bother me again.

That most beloved of all school subjects, PE, was another sore point for me. I, like a lot of other autistic people, have very poor co-ordination, something proven by the fact it took me far, far too long to learn to ride a bike. Beyond that though, I was very unfit, and lessons didn't focus on working on that. Instead, it seemed that each lesson was just an exercise in humiliation for those of us who weren't the elite few who could catch a ball or run fast. My anxiety went berserk (more so) the days I had PE, to the point where my psychiatrist had to write a letter and get me excused from lessons entirely. It was a wonderful reprieve, and a small glimmer of hope in an otherwise increasingly gloomy world.

Unfortunately, it meant I spent the time I would have been in PE with my form teacher who, after a traumatic experience on holiday, seemed...different. More vindictive, more angry with me. She would try to force me to eat, she would berate me for the smallest things. She called me manipulative on more than one occasion, and after one panic attack had left me cowering in her office, she called me a 'sad little girl with no friends'.

It was Sports Day, and I had the flu for the first time in my life. I felt absolutely dreadful, my head was full of the worst kind of gunk and I just wanted to sleep or handily slip into a coma until I felt better again. But I had to go into school, so my mum drove me in and dropped me off with a bottle of iced water. I must have looked ill because, not even an hour later, the receptionist didn't even consult my form teacher before calling my mum to ask her to pick me up. We got home, and again, we couldn't have been there very long at all before my mum got an angry phone call from my form teacher demanding I 'come back to school this instant' and participate. Clutching my now slightly sweaty iced water, I was driven back to school, where, in full school uniform I was forced to sit on the freezing playground tarmac and watch as people played netball. Again, I must have looked very ill, because I asked if I could go to the office and go home (I remember just feeling like death). I didn't hold out much hope, but I was sent to the office and the receptionist had to trudge across the muddy playing field in her kitten heels (*good*, I thought to myself, *get muddy feet*) to where my form teacher was holding court over some match or another. I guess, exasperated at me and without time to do anything else, she allowed me to be sent home. My mum was phoned again, and she soon arrived. She told me to go sit in the car and went back to the office. She's never told me exactly what she said to the receptionist, for dragging me in and out of school twice in one day, but I know it was far from complimentary. It was getting beyond a joke, and I think she was getting to the end of her tether. I spent the next few days off school sniffling and feeling very sorry for myself.

One time, after last lesson, I was in my form teacher's classroom with my friends, packing up to go home when I thought I heard her say something to me. I didn't catch it, and when I looked round she had gone through to the adjoining classroom. I glanced at my friends and they hadn't caught it either, so I put it from my mind and left to go home.

When I got home I was greeted by my very angry mum, who had received a phone call from my form teacher telling her that I'd deliberately ignored her request to disassemble an ironing board and had left the classroom laughing. I explained that I hadn't heard her, and that even if I had I would have had no idea how to collapse an ironing board (millennials, eh?). My mum's anger abated, but I still had to write a letter of apology to the teacher, even though as far as I could see I'd done nothing wrong.

Things were coming to a head, and as the last few months of year eleven approached, everything fell apart spectacularly.

ghosts

There's a reunion of ghosts in my head. I carry them with me wherever I go, wind whisper voices telling me to brush my teeth or stop telling lies. They treat me like a child and I bury my head beneath the duvet to hide from them. Because if they can't see you, they're not really there, you see? Except they're always there and where they are I am. I am ten years ago, I am twenty years ago, I am trapped in ice and watching as my breath fogs another memory. How can anyone survive the ripping of their bones? How can anyone sleep when the ghosts howl beside their bed? I cannot trick the ghosts by pretending they do not exist. They do not care for my thoughts.

They think they know what is best for me and that is to listen carefully sit up straight and for god's sake grow up.

I've lived and died and I think I'm part ghost myself and I think that's why they like me. They watch me as I smile at my newest nephew and they leave reminders in my brain that they have not forgotten and nor should I. They have ruled for the centuries I have seen, and maybe they have been defeated, dethroned or died, but you cannot kill a ghost, you can only find a way to stop grieving its loss—and how to stop grieving when the loss is of yourself? I do not have answers though I have given several.

The ghosts have no doubt murmured among themselves—will they leave now or stay a while longer? Do you think you carry every ghost, that everyone carries every ghost until they are more ghost than man? I wonder if I am as see-through as I feel. I am turning pale and the air is cold.

There is a window and there is a world, but it is not my

window and not my world. Maybe I did die. Maybe I haunt these grounds as readily as the ghosts I carry.

But haven't I proven that I am blood and flesh and bone time and time again? The ghosts cannot be heard except when they speak through me. If I silence them, I need not silence myself I just need to think around their words. If I am still more man than ghost some kind of being with lungs and the beating of a heart, then how can I be a memory. I am present, I am here, and for as long as I bleed, I can haul this body forwards.

There is a photo on the wall and it is a photo of love.

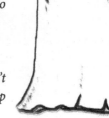

I think the ghosts are envious of it. They mutter around it trying to comprehend it. They are stripped back to almost nothing. Their power is in who they were and how I let them linger.

There is a photo on the wall.

The ghosts—

The ghosts aren't in it. They can't touch it. They try but their fingers slip through.

I took that photo.

If I can capture something untouched and untouchable by the ghosts—

if—

maybe—

maybe there is a part of me that still burns red hot. They have surrounded me with their chill but there is still a warmth to me.

The ghosts don't like that idea. They want me to be cold like them. But I don't want to be, not yet.

Oh, they are angry now!

But I hear my name spoken by the living far more than the dead and I hear it spoken with love and not disdain or hatred. If the ghosts had wanted to woo me they should have tried a little kindness. I am so susceptible to a gentle word.

There is a photo on the wall. It shows two soft souls and a moment. I took that photo. I am the ghost behind the lens. But then I was not haunting I was smiling and my heart was beating.

There is a photo on the wall.

I am not ready for a eulogy just yet. Clear my mouth of the dirt you've sprinkled over my body, I want to get up. I have so much more to be and the hours tick tock away.

Let the ghosts watch as I run. See if they can catch me.

There is a photo on the wall.

The worst days

2005

One day, I was sat in a maths class when I got a feeling of intense dread. To someone who doesn't know what a panic attack is, it just feels like you're dying. So I excused myself from the lesson and, crying with fear, made my way to the office, where the receptionist sent me on to my form teacher. She stood me in front of the class she was teaching and demanded I go back to my lesson. Her face started to swim in front of me and black scuds filled my vision. She grabbed me before I collapsed and dragged me into her office. Once there, she sat me down until the worst of it had passed. She reached for the phone. I thought she was going to let me go home. She rang my mum's number. She spoke to her for a minute, before hissing to me 'Tell your mum you're fine.' I didn't know what else to do...I was still crying, but I stammered out that I was fine. It seemed like an unnecessarily cruel punishment and as I left the office she added, 'Oh, and you've got eyeliner all down your cheeks, go wash it off.' If I had to choose just one thing that I could never forgive her for, it would be making me lie to my mum, gagging me from telling my mum how scared I was. I wish I could understand her logic, but I just can't.

The next day was an ordinary day, I was anxious, as usual, but it was okay, you know? I'd got used to it, and while it was awful, it wasn't new. It was morning break, and I was talking to my friends, when an awful feeling ran through me and I realised something was very, very wrong. I stumbled to the office and told the receptionist I needed to go home, right now.

And then my legs collapsed.

I sat against the wall for hours, my legs completely numb and immovable, without a hope of standing. I was terrified, I thought there was something seriously wrong. I was sure my mum would be called and I would be lifted into the car and taken to the hospital, where I would be put into a wheelchair to see the doctors who would try to figure out why half my body wasn't working. I waited and waited, glancing up every time a car pulled up. It was never my mum. My friends kept coming to visit me throughout the day and I would ask them to check at the office to see if my mum had been called. She hadn't, but my form teacher had.

And she was furious with me.

I've never seen anyone so angry with me. She stormed into the office and demanded that I stand. She said she would leave me for five minutes and if I wasn't standing by the time she got back there would be consequences. In retrospect, I don't know what she could have done to me, but I think at that point I was so afraid of her that I truly believed she might hurt me. Another pupil, sitting on a chair beside me, was lovely enough to cheer me on as I tried to arrange my legs into some semblance of standing. I eventually managed it, feeling like I was going to collapse at any moment, and when the form teacher came back she looked at me as if to say 'I told you so' and marched me to my final lesson of the day, English. I had been supposed to give an oral presentation at the front of the class about my favourite place, but I hadn't done it because I didn't *have* a favourite place, so maybe that's what triggered the panic attack. But my form teacher pulled my English teacher aside and told him in no uncertain terms that I was not to be allowed to leave the classroom. I spent the lesson listening to other people describe their favourite places and how happy they made them and considering the irony of it all. I was still convinced there was something physically wrong with me, and was terrified that my legs would never work properly again.

Finally, the lesson ended and on shaky, Bambi-like limbs I gathered up my stuff. My friends crowded around me and helped me walk home, the normally half-an-hour walk taking over an hour as I had to continually stop and regain my balance.

When I got home my mum was angry at me. I think she'd just reached a point where something had to give, and it had given. She'd made me an appointment to see the doctor the next morning (remember when that was possible? I'm really showing my age now). At that point, I didn't know who I could trust. I knew now that my form teacher was someone I was actively afraid of, and that she was trying to sow seeds of discord between my mum and me. I also knew that I couldn't stay at that school any longer.

The next day, the doctor listened to my story, and in a move I don't understand to this day, diagnosed me with depression. While I certainly *was* depressed, I don't really think he understood what was going on. Depressed people don't tend to randomly collapse. I was put on Prozac and sent back to school.

With nothing left to lose, I finally began to rebel.

when they ask

how do you explain anxiety to someone?
is it the hitch in your breathing and then
the tightness in your chest
as you try to catch yourself
and remind yourself that you're still standing
but your legs want to fold
and your brain is telling you that it's not safe
and you haven't been safe for a long time now
you can't remember what it felt like not to feel the gnaw
and you can't remember when it switched from
wanting not to cause a scene
to wanting to cause a scene
because if you collapse you get to leave
people will notice and care and treat you like spun sugar
but when you make your legs stride and your lungs burn
nobody is going to help you
and you'd cry if you had the air to do so
but instead you keep walking
and in that moment
you'd face a firing squad
because a bullet to the brain
is easier than meeting the eyes of a stranger

Study leave

2005

In the previous few months I'd fallen in with a group of friends who had little regard for teachers, rules or school. Weirdly, they'd been people who had previously bullied me and hated me, but it had been a misunderstanding—they'd been told I'd said something about them that wasn't true, and as rumours tend to do, it had escalated. We were friends now and hung out around school and sometimes after school at my house or a nearby park.

They told me how easy it was to just walk out of the school gates without anyone stopping you. It was a revelation. The first time I did it my heart was in my throat, and I thought I might throw up. But no teacher came running out after me, and I spent a leisurely couple of hours free and safe at the old railway, talking with my friends and just enjoying not being in school.

It's hard to fully put into words the freedom that came with walking away from what had become worse than any prison, away from a teacher whose word bound me to stay. Just walking out of the gates and knowing that she could not, even if she wanted to, drag me back, gave me hope. The façade was starting to crack, the idea of the authority figure being a kind of god was irreversibly damaged. Bunking off wasn't something I made a habit of, but damn, to know that I could was like discovering something utterly vital.

After the Worst Days, I took advantage of this more and more, sometimes with friends and sometimes on my own. My mum had reached a point where she had seemingly ascended to a level of calm about the whole situation where nothing I could do would surprise her, so more than once I'd phone her in the middle of the day from the phone box (showing my age again) around the corner from our house and tell her I was done for the day. I think in a way it was a relief for her. I don't think she ever got any grief for it from my teachers—I think they were all so used to me being absent from lessons that nobody thought to co-ordinate and track me down and tell my form teacher.

It was with this new attitude that I made a decision. It was the day before the Easter holidays, and I was sixteen years old, old enough to get a piercing. My friends had pierced my ears earlier in the year and I was already stretching them, but I wanted something that would get me kicked out of school, without a doubt. I'd always loved septum piercings ever since I'd first seen them on bmezine.com, and so I decided to go with that.

My mum and dad took me and my sister to the piercing studio, on a school day no less, and my dad and I went upstairs to get my septum pierced.

It hurt. I cannot tell you how much it hurt. I squeezed my dad's hand and flinched as the needle went through. When I opened my eyes, I could see the needle through my nose, and after another jolt of pain, the jewellery was in, a ring, something you certainly couldn't miss. Next, my sister got her nostril pierced.

With sore noses, we went home, and I enjoyed the Easter holiday, spending time with my friends and safe in the knowledge that should I go back to school, I wouldn't be there for very long.

Sure enough, I walked into school on the first day back, unafraid, back straight and garnering stares from other pupils. My friend in my form—a boy I had known since primary school, someone I'm deeply sad to have lost touch with, someone who was kind and gentle in a way few boys knew how to be—gave me a look and told me I was going to get into trouble, but I just shrugged. My form teacher walked in, and after sorting a few things on her desk, walked up to me. She hadn't noticed yet, in fact, she had a smile on her face. I'd won a poetry competition, she began to say, and had won £20 and publication, when suddenly she stopped—and said, I quote: 'I'm not even going to congratulate you now.'

I was hustled from the form room and she started yelling at me. 'Take it out,' she demanded repeatedly, 'take it out.' I couldn't, I replied, even if I wanted to. I wasn't going to. I'd never seen her so angry with me, but I felt calm. This was it. This was the last time I would have to deal with her. I'd done it. I was going to leave this place for good.

I was sent to the deputy head mistress's office, who again asked me to take it out, before asking why I hadn't just waited a few more weeks until exams were over. I refused to budge though, and my mum was called, and she came to pick me up. I couldn't stop the huge grin from breaking out on my face as I waited for her, and I realised that even though I was shaking, I was proud of myself. I'd stood up to my greatest bully and won. My mum took me home, and

I was only there for about ten minutes before she received another phone call. My sister's nose stud had been noticed by the same teacher. My mum was bemused and picked her up too, taking her to the studio to have it changed for a clear one, telling the teacher she'd taken it out.

My friends soon arrived at my house (remember this was probably 10am in the morning on a school day) and we spent the rest of the day at the beach (a five-minute walk away from my house), we got chips, and finally we meandered back to wait outside the school for the rest of our friends. I was just so happy and felt safe and free (I know I said that before but it bears repeating).

The next day my mum went up to the school and they hashed out a deal. As my septum ring obviously wasn't coming out, and as I was more trouble than I was worth at school, I was put on study leave until the exams. I picked up a few pieces of revision and left, my head held high. My nose hurt, but it was worth it.

Ironically, study leave is what saved my exam results in the end. Being able to study in a stress-free environment allowed me to learn without fear, without worrying that I was going to pass out. I spent most of my time on history, and a lot of time just bugging my mum until she told me to go and do my work, but it was great to be free of school for good. I wish I could have said goodbye properly to a lot of people I never saw again but needs must.

The only bad thing about study leave was that due to some rule I'm sure my form teacher cooked up, students on study leave couldn't attend prom. My dad and I had been dress shopping a couple of weeks before in Norwich, where he'd spent £70 on a beautiful dress I'd now never get to wear. For the next thirteen years, I'd long for an occasion to get the opportunity that had been stolen from me: to dress up pretty. I didn't realise it at the time, but that opportunity would be at the Saatchi Gallery, with my work on display.

So, with exams looming, and finally being able to catch my breath, I took a moment, and for a little while, things were okay.

Where are all the psychs?

You're probably reading this and wondering why the psychiatrists and psychologists weren't helping. We were seeing them at least once a week and had been since I was eight years old. As I mentioned before, I can't begin to count how many different ones I saw. As well as seeing professionally trained psychs, I also attended the charity, Mind. The staff there were very nice but didn't really know what to do for me as I had no official diagnosis. I had two mentors at school who mostly provided an excuse for not going to lessons and for me to catch a breather. But my mum was constantly on the phone to various professionals, begging for help, for anything. She told me later that she even asked if I could be taken in somewhere temporarily so I could be properly diagnosed and treated. The psychiatrist was horrified at the suggestion. At the time, I would have welcomed it.

The only diagnosis I got, apart from my diagnosis of depression after my panic attack, was one of social anxiety, which I had to suggest myself. The internet was getting more advanced, and I had taken to it like a moth to a flame. Around that time simple clicky-box personality tests were all the rage and posting your results on Myspace was the thing to do. I took one and scored really highly for social anxiety. The next time I saw my psychiatrist I brought it up, and she reluctantly agreed, though I could see she was humouring me. In my medical records she says that I 'seem[ed] to think I [had] social anxiety.'

As I mentioned earlier, there was no attempt made to look for a diagnosis of autism, it wasn't even suggested. I was just thought to be suffering from an 'adolescent crisis'. If it wasn't so damn depressing, it'd make me laugh at how incompetent the various psychiatrists, psychologists, mentors and so forth were, but the fact is thousands of people are still jumping through all these hoops every year desperately looking for answers and not receiving them.

I'm told that it's slightly easier now. A child I know was diagnosed a lot younger than I was (I was twenty-one) and is receiving much better help than I ever got, but that's because it's help tailored to autism and his co-morbids (co-morbidities are mental health problems that exist alongside the primary condition). I didn't have that. One of my medical records describes me as having gone 'from pillar to post', and that's pretty damn accurate.

My mum tried so hard, she was constantly on the phone and fighting my corner. We never thought to look up autism on the internet because we weren't aware of it as something that could be anything less than the terrifying portrayal it had in the media. But someone, one of the psychs, should have taken a step back and looked at the whole picture.

I can't forgive them that. It feels like an act of negligence.

Dad doesn't get it

One of the things my psychiatrist was supposed to set up while I was on study leave was that I wouldn't have to take my GCSEs due to some loophole he'd found which would allow the government to give me marks based on my predicted grades. This would have meant receiving the A's I had been predicted back before everything started going quite so pear-shaped. Unfortunately, this was a very old loophole and we didn't realise it no longer applied until the exams had already started and I'd missed some.

The decision was then whether to sit any exams at all. I chose to take the bare minimum to get into college, and it turned out to be one of the hardest things I've ever done.

My mum arranged that I would be put in a separate room for each of my exams, and that I could leave as soon as I was done. She would sit outside the room and read a book. It sounds ridiculously overblown, but there was no other way around it.

My dad drove us to the school, and as I vomited in the back seat on the way there, with my mum comforting me,

I wondered if he understood the cost of it.

My dad is older than my mum by a few years and wasn't around much when I was a child, through no fault of his own, but because he was working two jobs, as a musician and running an antiques shop. It meant he was always busy, and my mum raised us largely by herself. My dad never saw the worst of it, and never believed that there was anything wrong with me. If you'd asked him, he would have scoffed and said I was fine. Maybe it's a generational thing or maybe he was in denial, I don't know. Whatever it was, my mum later told me that it was during that car ride to school that it sank in for him that there was something wrong with me.

I knew I would fail the maths and science exams immediately upon opening the papers—not for lack of trying, but because I hadn't been able to learn. The last two vital years had been ones of survival, and I had clashed terribly with both teachers, falling further and further behind my peers until that crucial moment when I'd seen the first questions and known there was no way I could pass. I'd missed my English literature exam, but I sped through the English, media studies and history exams with ease. Those were the only exams I took.

On results day, I couldn't face going to the school to find out what I'd got. My mum had to go, and my friend came round afterwards. I was in bed, feeling sick (like, wow, something new and different for me there!). I got an A in English, media studies and history. I got a C in art. The rest I failed abysmally.

I was lucky that the college I wanted to go to still agreed to take me, on the proviso that I complete the Adult Numeracy Level 2 course my mum was taking at the same time. I went to one class, and looked over a bit of my mum's homework, but I have to admit I didn't take it too seriously. The time for the exam rolled around and I believe the paper was multiple choice, which made it much easier. I sped through the exam, worried about my mum who was sitting a table away. I kept glancing over at her, worried that she didn't seem to be getting as far through it as I had done, and at one point I even raised my hand to ask how much time we had left, just in case she was being too careful and losing time. I finished the exam and didn't really expect anything more to come of it.

A few weeks later, we got the results. Of all the people in the class, I was the only one who had passed. It had been the first time the tutor had taught Level 2 and she'd woefully underprepared the students for the exam. I felt gutted for my mum, and for the rest of the students, and amazed that I had somehow managed to pass despite being really, truly appalling at maths. But it was enough to get me into college.

I spent the last few weeks before college hanging out on a couple of occasions with my high school friends, dyeing my hair, and getting piercings. I'll talk about body modification more later, and how it's impacted my life, but for now let's just say I got a lot, and in fairly quick succession. It got to the point where my mum offered to get me a kitten if I stopped getting piercings—she was worried it was a form of self-harm. I did point out that actual self-harm would be a much cheaper option, but nevertheless I got my kitten, Sophia. I didn't stop getting piercings though, I never have.

As college grew nearer, I grew closer to one friend and further away from the rest of the group. I didn't really fit in, they smoked and drank and had sex, normal teenage things, and I just wanted to stay home on the internet and blog and make Youtube videos. In retrospect, they probably liked that my parents allowed them to do these things in the house, because as my mum would always say, she'd rather she knew where I was. I never partook, not on the urging of the boy I liked, nor any of the girls who seemed so much more, and effortlessly so, cooler than me. They were, in their way, bullies, though I don't think they'd recognise themselves as such. Certainly, they had bullied me, and when eventually they crossed lines I couldn't, they found new ways to torment me, the internet bulging ever bigger and more omnipresent, making remarks like they wished I would kill myself, or sharing private blogs for all to see. You see, even back then, I was a chronic over-sharer, though in the end, that's what's led you to reading these words, so I suppose I should be grateful for the practice.

Back to my dad though—he gets it now. After seeing what I went through to go to my exams, he became a properly overprotective papa bear, and made it his mission to get me out of the house, wrapping an arm around me when I went wobbly and getting me out of places when I needed to leave. I don't know if he fully understands me in the same way my mum does, but I'm very grateful to him for stepping up and being there for me. We're now closer than we've ever been, and I love hearing about his life, and dragging him along to conventions and concerts. We saw The Blockheads a couple of years back at Norwich Arts Centre and it was a great experience—he'd seen Ian Dury before he died, and now I'd seen the rest of the band with him. I was so anxious the entire time, but he held me up and kept me grounded, and afterwards he helped me get selfies with the band. That was pretty cool. They were a part of punk history and I'm glad I got to share that with him. And I'm glad he got to see my work in the Saatchi Gallery. I hope he's proud of me.

College

2005–2006

The first day of college didn't begin very well for me (oh wow, I bet you're so surprised). I was optimistic about a fresh start, but anxious as anything, and as we filed into the welcoming assembly I fiddled with my piercings and couldn't pay attention to anything that was being said.

After a few minutes, I had to get out. I just had to. I raised my hand and excused myself and sat outside on the grass for the rest of the assembly, hating myself.

I was going to be taking psychology, philosophy and sociology. My first class was sociology, and I still remember the first person I talked to there because I asked him if I was in the right class. And also because I would have a crush on him for the next few years.

I'd chosen sociology because the introduction class I'd attended when looking around the college had focused on feral children, something that both saddened and fascinated me. Actual sociology, though, turned out to be quite dull. The teacher was charismatic and lovely, and I was sitting beside someone I vaguely knew from going to the local

Battle of the Bands, so it was okay.

Next was psychology, and I was completely on my own. We had to go to the library and practice looking up references, and I felt so uncomfortable and anxious that I just wanted to go home.

Philosophy was better, and I got to hang out with my best friend in that class. Once again, it wasn't what I'd expected it to be from the introduction—we'd talked about *The Matrix* and I'd brought up an issue that had always bugged me: a character mentions that they look the same in the Matrix as they do in real life because of 'residual self-image', but how can you know what you look like if you've never seen yourself? It made the whole 'Matrix within a Matrix theory' seem credible, the idea that upon escaping one layer of the matrix the humans within the film merely entered another layer. But in reality, philosophy was a lot of listening to the teacher tell us how much he liked David Hume and trying to wrap our heads around the idea of Plato's Forms.

My counsellor from Mind was there at the end of the day to sort of debrief me—he was supposed to give me a lift home, but he didn't. I think more than anything he was just using me to get a foot in the door at the college, which was slightly disappointing.

After a couple of months, I moved tables in sociology and made friends with the first boy I'd talked to, and another boy, Mervyn, who I still talk to today (I'll talk about him later). I was crushing hard on the first boy, he was a stoner and would frequently come to class reeking and looking shifty and asking if you could smell it on him. I'd always assure him that you couldn't, but you definitely could.

I'd dropped psychology by now, so I was only taking the two classes. Even so, I was struggling a lot.

If you want to know the worst food to throw up every morning without fail, it's Coco Pops. I made a second home in the toilets and spent most of my college days camped out there. I missed a lot of classes and couldn't concentrate.

I stopped going into college in the half term before the end of the first year, so around Easter time. I got to sit my exams—I was put in a room on my own again and allowed to leave when I'd finished, and my dad sat in the car outside. I had no idea where to begin on my philosophy exam, so just magnificently failed it. I also had to take a general studies exam, and as I'd been excused from general studies lessons that was a bit of a nasty shock. I failed it, but I did the best I could. Out of all of them, the only success was my sociology exam. I scraped a C but I don't know how I managed that, to be honest.

I was growing ever more isolated, retreating to my room and not leaving the house at all. It was the beginning of my agoraphobia, what I refer to as my Lost Years. They would stretch from the age of seventeen to my late twenties. It's really upsetting to realise that I lost an entire decade to my anxiety and depression, but that's what happened.

We tried college again two years later, my last chance at free education. I took art and graphic design, hoping creative projects would be easier for me. I don't know why it never occurred to me to take English or English literature; I just don't think the confidence was there then. I lasted half a term the second time at college, I didn't know anyone, and my anxiety hadn't abated any, despite the cocktail of medication the psychs were throwing at me. It was easier to retreat, and at age nineteen I became almost completely housebound, leaving only for rare trips to the supermarket or to get tattoos.

That second exemption sounds strange, right? How could I get tattoos when my anxiety was so bad? Read on, my friend, and I'll try to explain a little more of the ol' Autism Logic.

Body modification

2005–2018

(I've been informed that this chapter isn't very interesting unless you're deeply into body modification, and even then, there's only so much you can hear about other people's tattoos. That said, a lot of autistic people have special interests, and body modification is one of mine. Special interests are the things we info dump on you about, the things we bore you with. So, in true autistic style, allow me, if you will, to info dump for two thousand words on something that's very, very important to me.)

My mum took me to get my first tattoos—the words 'Remember to feel real' on my wrists. I was a wreck and vomited in the tattoo parlour's bathroom afterwards (there's a very long list of 'unusual places I have vomited', including, but not limited to, my uncle's first brand new car). My mum had gotten her first tattoo a few years before, an old-fashioned heart with the family's initials in the scroll.

Seeing musicians covered in tattoos made me realise I wanted that. There was something so beautiful about it and the idea that you could literally carry your interests around with you wherever you went like a roadmap of your personality was amazing to me.

I discovered bmezine.com, a body modification website, and spent hours every day going through the galleries. It opened my eyes to things I could never have imagined—scarification, tongue splitting, suspension, as well as having galleries upon galleries of pictures of tattoos and piercings.

After getting my septum pierced, I went on to get my bottom lip pierced three times, in the middle and on the sides, and my upper lip pierced twice, on the sides. I got my anti-eyebrow pierced and my inverse navel. And then I got my cheeks pierced.

I know nowadays everyone and their grandmother has their cheeks pierced, but at the time it was still a very new concept and I was only the second person my piercer had ever done it on. I wrote up an article about my experience for bmezine and was lucky enough to get it published on the front page, which was a big deal at the time. I loved my cheek piercings, but they're a piercing that is notoriously difficult to heal, so I had to remove them. The scars they left gave me dimples, which I think are pretty darn cute.

I also got my tongue pierced, but that lasted for less than a day. It hurt like anything, more than I could have imagined, and the feeling of having a foreign object in my mouth was just awful. I couldn't eat with the pain and so the next morning I went back to the piercer and had it removed. It was an instant relief.

At some point or another I've had pretty much everything above the waist pierced—I'm a pretty useful gauge for whether something's going to hurt or not.

I stretched my ears to thirty-three millimetres which is about an inch and a half, but sleeping on them and trying to find jewellery that wouldn't irritate them (even the most inert stone jewellery would make them itchy and irritable) eventually became too much of a hassle and I had to make a choice. Rather than have my ear lobes reconstructed (because I know I have the willpower of...someone with no willpower and would immediately stretch them again as soon as they were healed), I chose to have an earlobe removal instead. I've not seen many of these around, there's only one person I follow on Instagram that I've noticed, but it doesn't look out of place. If you didn't know I had it, you wouldn't comment on it. I missed my stretched lobes a lot, I'd had them from when I was fifteen to the age of twenty-seven, so they'd become a huge part of me and learning about different stones and picking out jewellery was always fun. But I had to move on for my own comfort.

Something unusual I got done was my magnet implant. Magnet implants are typically placed in the top of the finger, behind the squishy pad. I was so anxious before the procedure and running on no sleep whatsoever, the anxiety having kept me up all the night before. I had to look away for the entire time as first the needle and then the tiny magnet were inserted, but it worked immediately, and I was able to pick up paper clips with my finger, the magnet working through the skin. It was really, really cool. When I got home, I realised I could feel the magnetic fields coming from the microwave, the magnet would vibrate, and it became like a sixth sense as much as a party piece. Unfortunately, the magnet started to reject through no fault of the practitioner's, and it had to be removed. I definitely want to get another magnetic implant, but maybe in a part of my body that doesn't see such frequent movement.

Tattoos, though—tattoos were the bug that really bit me.

If you've seen a photograph of me you'll have noticed I'm pretty well covered, it's been a long eleven years of work and cover-ups and laser removal to get to this point and I'm nowhere near done. Autism Logic means I don't always make the best decisions. For example, blacking out my left arm was a huge mistake and I shouldn't have done it—it's valuable real estate that I can no longer use as I would have liked, and right now it's not looking so great, but I'm planning to get it fixed soon and hopefully get some white work put over the top of it.

My favourite tattoo isn't big or ostentatious, it's my Bucky Bear on my left leg, just below my knee. It's about an inch and a half long, but it reminds me of Bucky Barnes, someone who is hugely important to me and who I'll talk about more later.

Without a doubt, my most painful tattoo was my stomach. It's the only tattoo I've had to tap out on and go back to with numbing cream. It's a beautiful piece though, now it's finished, a mandala that stretches from my belly button right up to just below my sternum.

You're probably wondering about my face tattoos, and you're right to. There's a *lot* of stigma attached to face tattoos, for reasons I don't really understand, but then I've never looked at a tattooed person and thought they looked scary except for the white pride nationalists with their swastikas and Union Flags. I have four face tattoos, well, technically a few dozen more than that. Let me explain—I have fake freckle tattoos. I know, I know, you're probably rolling your eyes because for some reason people find that so incredibly lame. People normally get them done with temporary inks, but no way was I paying for something that would only last six months, so after a lot of experimentation, my tattoo artist and I found a mix of permanent inks that would look relatively natural on my face (my tattoo artist puts up with a lot). They don't look perfect, but I love them. My other, more traditional face tattoos are a watercolour moon curving around my right eye in the shape of a 'C' for Charlotte. It's also the American sign language symbol for 'moon', which I thought was really cool. I have two crossed arrows on the left side of my face, to celebrate meeting Norman Reedus at Walker Stalker Con 2016. And the anchor below my left eye, which was my first face tattoo. I got this at a very delicate time in my life, when the depression was eating me up. I'd written a blog post I'd never published, and referred to my nephew as my anchor, the one thing definitively holding me here. So I got it in the place I would see it the most—right on my face, to remind me of him.

You wouldn't even notice my last face tattoo unless you were looking for it. It's a white line going through my lip on the left side, to look like a scar. I'd originally wanted it done in scarification, but my practitioner was nervous about doing it and I don't scar well either. Any stitches I've ever received have healed to nothing, and I didn't want to go through a procedure like that and not see any results. Why a scar, you ask? Because I felt like I'd been through so many battles in my life and, because none of them had been physical, I had nothing to show for it. I wanted a subtle reminder that I was a fighter, even if my battle was largely internal. And as I couldn't exactly tattoo my kidneys, that was the choice I made instead.

There's something I've always loved about being a tattooed person that other tattooed people hate: people tend to avoid you and think you're somehow scary if you have tattoos. It's a dumb misconception, obviously. I'm five foot two and have the upper body stretch of a newborn baby, but I get stink eye from people as I walk around, especially if they notice my face tattoos—people actively avoid me. It's nice for that to be the first thing people notice about me rather than my autism. I don't want to wear my autism all the time, but unfortunately, I have to. My tattoos are like a sheet of armour I can put over the top of that, a distraction from the way I can't quite make eye contact or that I'm shaking a little too much. It's a conversation starter, especially these days when so many people have got a tattoo, and it's just nice to be thought of as 'the girl with all the tattoos' before 'the girl with autism'.

You may be wondering how I managed to get tattoos, especially when I had agoraphobia (which I still do, to a degree). To me, tattoo parlours are the safest places outside of my own home. If I had to pick one place to go to and spend an entire day, it would be a tattoo parlour. While there is a whiff of elitism in certain parlours, for the most part, they are unpretentious, and tattoo artists don't judge. I've met a few mean ones in my time, and indeed a few racist ones, but by and large, tattoo artists are some of the nicest people you're ever likely to meet. They may look scary sometimes, but they can be really lovely, and when you consider how intimate their job is, they kind of have to be.

Even so, to this day I still get incredibly anxious every single time I get a tattoo. It doesn't get any easier. I've probably had over a hundred hours of tattooing done in my life, but I still freak out the night before and the day of the tattoo. I just have to find coping mechanisms, like listening to music—choosing an album I know really well so I have some semblance of predictability and distraction from the pain. Numbing cream—I know some people think it's for wimps, but honestly, if I have the option to be in pain or not be in pain, I'm going to choose the latter and I don't care what that does to my street cred. Finally, tattoos are great because most pieces are done by the hour, which means you have a fixed time slot and it can't really deviate from that because other people are booked in. When worst comes to worst and I think I can't handle much more, whether it's because of the pain or the anxiety, I just count down the minutes in five-minute stretches.

And a tattoo, unless like me you're prone to poor life choices and seek out the laser, lasts a lifetime. An hour's discomfort is entirely different from having to go to the supermarket to buy food which, while it will keep you alive, is only temporary. A tattoo you can look at time and time again, and it becomes a part of you. I've never said that about a loaf of bread.

The lost years

I talked earlier about the lost years, when my agoraphobia got the better of me and left me housebound except for trips out maybe once a month. It's really hard to put into words what it's like to spend every single day indoors doing nothing. I know that sounds like blessed relief to some people, like, how lucky am I that I had nothing that needed to be done and no responsibilities, but the truth is that it's so incredibly isolating and damaging to your mental health that I wouldn't wish it upon anybody.

I think a lot of people believe agoraphobia doesn't really exist, and that's because it is such an invisible mental illness. If you have agoraphobia and are referred to a psychologist, you're not going to be able to go to your appointments, that's the nature of the beast. So the system fails you and you fall through the net. I can't imagine how many people are living like this, stuck at home with nothing to do all day but watch television or browse the internet, longing for any kind of interaction, or at worst, the sweet release of death. It drags you down—you lose touch with everyone you've known, and you lose any sense of self-esteem you might have built up over the years. You lose touch with popular culture and what's 'hip' and current. Only so much can be experienced through the lens of online media. To really experience and absorb life, you have to exist within it, and that's incredibly difficult to do when you have the same four walls, the same view outside the window, and the same people around you every single day.

You begin to resent everything: yourself, your family, the people online whose lives you watch and envy. How can they think so little of going out and spending a day at the beach? Don't they realise how lucky they are?

I've missed out on so much, so many milestones. I've never kissed anyone, never had a relationship, never been drunk (not that I'd want to drink, or could with my medication, but still), never learnt to drive (again, I don't want to, but the option would have been nice). My dreams of going to university were shattered and, given that I'd dedicated my entire childhood to that one solid goal, it broke my heart.

As my brother and sister both grew up, and I saw them living their own lives and having their own adventures, it started to really hammer home what a failure I was. As I watched my brother finish college and start university, I wanted to tear my skin off in disgust with myself. I tried to feel happy for him, but mostly I just felt so angry at my own brain. When he graduated there was no way I could have attended the ceremony, but what's worse, it sent me deeper into that black hole of depression. It's really hard to stay positive when every day is exactly the same. It looks like there's no way out. I'm going to talk about that time now, and then I'm going to talk about how to survive it.

eulogy

i died, and nobody noticed
i picked out a tombstone
and a small patch of earth
a rectangle of dirt
ready to reclaim me

i died, and nobody noticed
i picked out a funeral suit
and made up invitations
embossed on recycled card
the last poem i would write

i died, and nobody noticed
i rested beside the roots of a tree
feeling the soil calling to me
the autumn leaves crisp against bare feet
they buried me with dirty fingernails

i died, and nobody noticed
a small jukebox skipped its way through 'hallelujah'
and i sang along even though they didn't hear
and i thought of all the chords i knew
and wondered which one david played

i died, and nobody noticed
i was the ash on your tongue
the dust in your eyes

your face contorted
and you did not cry

i died, and nobody noticed
which is why, i think
it makes it so easy
to push through the oak of the lid
and step into the moonlight,
a small whisper of a ghost

it has rained since i was gone.

The blackest days

2006–2018

I've always called my depression 'circumstantial depression', though that's probably a bit whimsical for what it is. I think I am prone to depression naturally, genetically, but my circumstances definitely haven't helped matters.

Depression isn't sadness, as it's often portrayed, though there is that too—mostly it's numbness. You don't care if you live or die. If you got hit by a bus tomorrow, it'd be a blessed relief because then at least it would be *over*.

It's a hole your brain digs for you and, every day, instead of calling for a rope, it digs another foot deeper. You forget what the sunlight feels like on your skin and you become a husk of a person, utterly devoid of anything. Things that once made you happy now leave you indifferent.

It's hard to put into words. It's a lack of something vital, as though something that burns inside you has been snuffed out.

You'll sleep a lot, because you want the days to be over quicker. You won't eat, because eating seems like an elaborate decadence wasted on a body you won't be using for much longer anyway. You won't shower, because showering requires too much planning: choosing clean clothes, turning the shower on, getting undressed, actually showering, and then getting dry and putting clothes on again. You won't clean because the effort seems monumental. You just exist, in a gradually more stinky and greasy state, hating yourself because your head is itchy and there's stuff everywhere and there's nothing you can do about it.

On more than one occasion I have been sure I was going to kill myself. I had dates set in my head and a foolproof method. I won't go into details about that because that seems irresponsible, and I don't want to trigger anyone. But the idea had been planted, and it felt like taking a deep breath after being underwater for a long time.

My mum admitted to me that she hated to come into my room in case one day I just wouldn't wake up. I didn't know what to do. There's a line in a Robbie Williams song that sums it up—'I don't wanna die, but I ain't keen on living either'. I'm sure it's been said in a thousand different ways, but it still rings true. Being depressed doesn't necessarily mean you *want* to die, it just seems like the easiest option, not just for yourself, but for your family.

You convince yourself they'd be better off without you. That you're dragging them down. That you're a burden and that without you they could flourish. Sure, they'd be sad at first, but soon you'd just be a memory, something that hurts on occasion but that they can survive and live through.

The irony is that depression is exactly the same. It hurts, but you'll live through it.

Re-engaging with life was one of the hardest things I ever did. I had become so used to being stagnant, inert, that to get the ball rolling again required every ounce of strength I had, and it was such a slow process that to the outsider looking in it wouldn't have been noticeable. It took years, and there were definite setbacks. There are still times when I fall into that black hole, but now I have better coping mechanisms, people I can reach out to and activities I can passively take part in, like watching certain movies, certain stand-up shows, listening to certain music, finding things to look forward to.

That last point is vital. Depression makes it seem like you don't have a future beyond where you are. That you'll be in the hole forever. You have to believe that one day you'll be out of the hole and doing something you enjoy. Make plans. They may seem impossible, you may feel like you'll never be able to achieve them, but book those concert tickets or find a movie you can't die without seeing. If you follow a book series, pre-order the next instalment. You need to keep on living, even if the cost seems too much sometimes.

You're allowed to have down days, when everything is too much. Take care of yourself, don't beat yourself up. But remember that every time you wanted to quit before, you survived. And you will do again.

Diagnosis

2009–2010

I got diagnosed by sheer fluke. My psychologist was visiting the house and things were bad. A few days before my mum had just happened to watch a documentary on the BBC about autistic people trying to find jobs and she had noticed the similarities between how I behaved and they behaved. She was the first person to ever diagnose me with autism. She mentioned it to the psych who said hurriedly, 'well, that would have been our next course of action.' Yeah, right.

The first things I had to do were the Autism Quotient and Empathy Quotient tests. I mentioned the Autism Quotient test really early on, you probably remember it and maybe even looked it up and took it. I guess I passed (or failed, I'm not quite sure on the terminology), because my assessment continued and next I had to try to recognise faces.

It's the most tedious thing in the world, sitting in front of a laptop older than time itself and trying to figure out what emotion Photoshopped faces are supposed to be displaying. It was impossible. I don't look at people's faces if I can avoid it, so I failed (or passed) that test magnificently.

Finally, I had to take an IQ test. There's a common misconception that autistic people don't speak or aren't very articulate. It goes along with the mistaken belief that there are high and low functioning autistic people. This is such a frustrating thing, because every one of us is both high and low functioning depending on the circumstances. Sit me in front of a computer and ask me to write a story and I'll be as eloquent as you like. Ask me to leave the house and there'll be claw marks on the door frames. The IQ test was a mix of memory and vocabulary questions, as well as spotting differences and maths problems, and a bit of general knowledge too. For the final test, I had to solve a set of puzzles of random shapes, and quite by accident (or was it design? I'll never know) the person administering the test left the solutions within my range of vision, so I aced that. So, my official IQ might be a couple of points higher than it should be, but I think cheating and getting away with it shows a certain level of ingenuity.

Anyway, I came away with a score of 118, which is not genius level by any stretch of the imagination but is slightly above average. In the vocabulary test, however, I scored within the ninety-second percentile, meaning I was in the top eight per cent of people who...know words. That both was and wasn't surprising, I mean, people have always said I'm good with words, but they always feel clumsy on my tongue, and I hate watching myself speaking on video (oh irony, I hear you cry).

Anyway, in January of 2010, I was officially diagnosed with Asperger's (Asperger's now falls under the DSM definition of ASD—Autism Spectrum Disorder, rather than being its own sub-category). At first, I was really angry at the diagnosis: at least with anxiety it's something fixable, with enough therapy and drugs. Autism meant the problem was my brain itself, incurable, forever. But at the same time, it came with acceptance from my mum, my dad, my brother and sister. Everyone who knew me suddenly understood me a whole lot better. My mum, especially, made it her mission to learn as much about the condition as possible, and she'd be reading a book, or we'd be watching a programme on television and she'd go 'that's you.' And it would be me.

Once you know what you're looking for, it's obvious.

After being diagnosed, I was immediately offered cognitive behavioral therapy (CBT), but it was too fresh, too raw to take on straight away. Having refused that though, it seemed like I was being difficult, and I imagine the psychiatrist drew a heavy breath and sighed because I wasn't co-operating as he would have liked.

I won't disparage the ailing NHS too much, but after being diagnosed and the initial offer of CBT, there wasn't much that was put on the table. The suggestion was made that I attend City College Norwich, an hour away from where I live, which would require me to get the train there and back every day and blend in with the sixteen-year-olds—despite being twenty-one, and agoraphobic. I was also too old to qualify for free further education, and there was no government funding available to help me pay for college. I was exasperated. It seemed like even the psychiatrist didn't understand.

My care co-ordinator was a weird one. Every time I saw her, I was struck with an overwhelming desire to buy her a new pair of trainers because hers looked so raggedy and old. And she wasn't that helpful. She wouldn't get back to us half the time, and was patronising as anything, speaking in placating tones without really taking on board what we were saying.

For a while, I had the most excellent social worker. She tried so hard to find me things to do and ways to become more active and social. She got me the opportunity to help out at a local tattoo studio and, though my anxiety rarely allowed for it, it was an amazing experience. But all too soon, she switched jobs, because being a social worker was too stressful. I don't blame her in the slightest.

Right now, I hang in a state of limbo. I'm supposed to be referred to a psychologist to start some kind of therapy, but I'm not sure what and when. It's been two years and we've made no progress on that front. The area I live in is chronically underfunded, and the psychiatrist who had actually trained in autism has left to work for another trust. Now there is no autism specialist in the area, and that leads to frustration all round, as both sides try to get their point across and neither understands the other fully. As I write this, I don't know what they can offer to 'fix' me. I think I just got really, really lucky that Spectrum came along at just the right time and I was finally ready to help myself. The NHS is an invaluable resource, and if it's eventually torn to shreds we will miss it, but as it is, the help and resources just aren't out there for autistic people. There aren't enough people trained to recognise it and if it hadn't been for my mum flicking to a random television channel one evening, I still might not be diagnosed.

(A note: at the time of editing I have been discharged from the care of the psychiatric team as 'there is nothing more [they] can do for me'.)

Fandom

Fandom saved me. Fandom made me a writer. Fandom was there when real life was too harsh to be a part of. When school felt suffocating and home was not the retreat I had hoped for, logging onto the internet and reading and writing and just being a part of this decentralised, demonetised creative experience was immensely freeing.

I found fandom at a young age, while searching for Harry Potter related stuff on the internet. Fandom, and in particular, fan fiction, was mind-blowing to me. People were taking established stories and expanding on them, making them better, taking them in new directions, and adding much-needed diversity. I was immediately hooked.

I know fan fiction is looked down upon as being 'all porn', but that couldn't be further from the truth. True, there is a lot of smut floating around, but there are deeper stories too. Fan fiction is a way to talk about things you can't talk about in real life—sexuality, gender, mental illness, abuse, all of the taboo subjects that you can't bring up at a dinner party. It is deeply healing to those who both write and read it.

I never really wrote fan fiction (except maybe three thousand words of *Sherlock* fan fiction during the first series) until after I saw *Captain America: The Winter Soldier*. After watching the movie, I immediately raced to my favourite site and searched desperately. I needed to know what happened next to Steve Rogers (Captain America) and Bucky Barnes (the Winter Soldier). I needed worlds upon worlds where things were slightly, or massively, different. And I found them.

I haven't really talked about my own sexuality thus far because, to be honest, it's not something that gets any airtime in my real life, but I'm bisexual. And finding people writing LGBT+ characters in fan fiction was so refreshing. And something about Steve and Bucky's dynamic just grabbed me and they quickly became my OTP (one true pairing).

I read everything and anything, and I found I related to Bucky in a way I hadn't related to any fictional character before. He was a good man who had suffered tremendously. And everyone wanted him to have a happy ending. He'd have to earn it, and a lot of the stories focused on recovery and what that would entail, and as someone who was on the cusp of really trying to get better, this was invaluable to me. I won't name specific stories I read, but one in particular stood out and as I read it and read about Bucky's recovery, I honestly believed that I too could recover one day and be a proper human being again.

I wondered if I could write about Bucky and Steve too.

I watch a lot of Youtube, and one channel in particular, vlogbrothers, I've watched for years. John Green is one half of the vlogbrothers and an author, and he gave a piece of advice on writing that I've never forgotten—'Give yourself permission to suck.' He meant—get the damn words on the page and fix them later. Just get them down. You're not going to be great straight away, but you'll get there. Everything you read, everything you write, it's all practice and it's making you a better writer. This goes for any artistic discipline, but I applied it to writing, and it worked.

My first story was a short thousand-word piece wondering about Bucky coming home and realising that Steve had never properly built a home for himself, that he was living in a house rather than a home. Over the course of the story I had Bucky turn it into a home for the two of them.

My next story was a fifty-thousand-word epic, with another fifty-thousand-word sequel, updated every day. I still can't believe I wrote that, and it doesn't exist online any more (I hope). It wasn't very good, but it proved something to me I hadn't realised before—that I had the discipline to write and the ability to do so. And people seemed to like my writing as well.

From there I started to draw on my own experience with trauma, anxiety, depression, even autism—anything and everything I could think of. I also wrote about subjects that I thought were important, like being transgender, suffering from an eating disorder, and what if the world ended? Also vampires. I have a soft spot for vampires. I read *The Vampire Chronicles* at a very impressionable age and love writing about them now.

My favourite story was one of the last I wrote—with Bucky as a musician and Steve as his long-lost muse. It didn't receive as much love as I had hoped it would, but to me it felt like a real story, something real authors would write. I felt proud of it. It was only seventeen thousand words long, but it contained an entire world, and with Bucky as its central character, I soon realised I was writing him as autistic.

I'd never done this before, and only one person picked up on it, asking if he was on the spectrum, but for me it was ground-breaking. It felt like writing myself, I gave him my anxiety, my depression. Of course, the Bucky in the story was far more talented than I'd ever be, but he had a bunch of my own insecurities and fears shoved into his brain.

I know it sounds dumb to find solace in fictional characters. Maybe you're under the impression than fan fiction isn't real writing, that because it's based on something else it's somehow less valid.

Let me tell you—these writers aren't getting paid. They're writing because they love to do it. Because they have stories they want or need to tell. It's pure and honest and without pretence. At the end of chapters students will apologise for being late to update because they had exams. In fact, pretty much everyone I've read has apologised for not updating quickly enough. *They're not getting paid*. They do this because these characters mean something to them. Mean everything to them.

If that isn't what writing should be about, then I don't know what is.

But I want to add a note of caution. It isn't all sunshine and rainbows in the world of fandom. There are people out there who delight in and take perverse pleasure from writing the most abhorrent of stories, and there are websites which will protect them, and indeed, people who will protect them. Like an ouroboros eating itself, any argument made against frank depictions of some truly horrific acts are met with outrage, as though the person who is appalled is in the wrong. It's a mess, quite frankly, and best left well alone, or at the very least, approached with a blacklist of every conceivable filtered tag you can think of already in place, and then some.

Some people, and there is probably a Venn diagram of the people I'm about to mention and the people I just mentioned, use fanfiction purely as a way to fetishise gay men and their relationships, and to prescribe heteronormative roles to their relationships. 'Who is the woman in the relationship?' they will cry, when of course, the answer, is 'there isn't one, that's the whole point.' I believe this degree of fetishising is why fanfiction has such a bad reputation, and is merely seen as porn, rather than as a way to explore writing in a free and welcoming space.

I mention these points not to damage the community, but as things that have bothered me personally, as an autistic and queer person. It's sometimes easy when you're writing to forget that your words have a real-world effect on the people who are reading them, which is why representation is so important in media. But this goes both ways. When we look into the mirror and what we see written is distorted and wrong, it can affect us, and our perception of ourselves and others. While it's easy to say fiction has no impact on reality, I do not believe that to be true. I believe art in every form is more powerful than we believe and should be wielded with great responsibility.

Fake friends
(internet intimacy)

2018

The internet is a marvellous tool for autistic people to use to make friends. In fact, it was practically designed for us, and almost certainly designed because of us (high five to all the autistic folk working in computing!). We can be as anonymous as we choose, we can infodump as much as we like on forums as niche as we are. The internet is big enough to encompass us perfectly, so we should all be able to shuffle along nicely, right?

I have found that the internet is a lot like an eternal high school. There are social rules to be followed, and everyone is still vying for popularity points. You can keep to yourself, but if you want friends you will still need to start a conversation.

I'm not saying you can't make very real friends on the internet. Because you can. Definitely. But I am going to recount an experience I had, not so long ago, as a warning.

We met through mutual interests. We talked and though they were younger than me and tended to talk about quite disturbing content sometimes, they helped me with my writing and it was fun to goof off with them. We had in-jokes, you know? So, okay, they would ruin my birthday with carefully orchestrated stunts, confessing their love to me whilst drunk despite knowing that was a line I would never cross, but the next day we would be back to normal. I stayed up until 5am chatting to them, we would Skype, even though I could never hear them properly because they refused to turn the television down.

They had a lot of problems, that much was clear, and being younger than me, were less inclined to listen to advice (fair enough, who wants to listen to advice when you can listen to your impulses?). Everything was a drama, all the time. I never knew how much was real or fake, exaggerated or whether they were in real danger. I was constantly worried about them, but I counted them as my best friend. We made vague plans for me to fly to their country one day, or for them to fly here.

I felt like I knew them as though I'd grown up with them. We'd exchanged letters and gifts and it felt as though it could be twenty years later, and we'd still be joking about the same old things. I think perhaps that was where the rot set in— neither of us was moving forwards.

It was my friend's birthday, and I went all out, spending hundreds of pounds on carefully chosen presents, wrapping them up in a huge box that cost an absolute fortune to courier overseas, and then I waited. We had a thing about opening our presents to one another on camera, so I awaited their video. The messenger service we used was notoriously terrible for actually notifying you when you had a message, so I didn't receive the upload link until late afternoon. The first thing I noticed about the video was that the television was on, so not only could I not hear a thing my friend was saying (something I'd repeatedly brought up with them) but also, they kept glancing away to watch it, as though my presents were just...not very interesting. I watched them open everything and they just...didn't seem to care. They took each item out and duly looked at it before putting it aside. When the video ended, I realised they hadn't said thank you.

After that, we didn't really talk much. I wondered if maybe they'd been hanging on for the gift, like some kind of deadline. I thought, well, that was an expensive lesson to learn.

Then the anonymous hate mail started arriving in my online inbox.

It was too specific to be from anyone else. It referenced things we'd talked about privately. It had to be from them. The messages implored me to kill myself.

If there's a moral to this story, it's this: there are really good people on the internet. The love of your life could be one click away. But there are also people who will see your loneliness and exploit it. Who will turn on you and because of their own issues, try to make you hurt the way they hurt. If you feel this is happening, and I'm not talking to you just if you're a teenager, but if you're an adult too—literally anyone is vulnerable to this—take a step back. People can promise you the world. And maybe they mean it at the time. But because of the way our brains are wired, we'll take that promise at face value and give it more weight than someone who isn't autistic. I don't know what the answer is to this. Just, tread carefully, friends. It may be a lesson you have to learn for yourselves. But dammit if it doesn't hurt to do so, even if you're forewarned.

Conventions

I went to my first convention in 2015: Nor-Con (Norfolk Convention), with my brother. I cosplayed as America Chavez from the Marvel comics, having spent hours painstakingly putting together her iconic jacket. Only one person recognised me; they were also dressed as a Young Avenger, and the convention itself was tiny, held in only two rooms with little space for mingling or even moving. There wasn't much to see or do, but it was a start. Just being around people who were so enthusiastic about fandom and all that it entailed, dressing up and being unashamedly geeky was amazing, and I felt like I'd found my people. I'd been to tattoo conventions and felt so much more out of place. No, fandom conventions were where I belonged.

In March of 2017, I went to Walker Stalker Con, a convention based around the show *The Walking Dead* (a show whose premise is basically 'the world has ended and there are zombies and then things just keep getting worse—forever'). It was my first big convention and I had no idea what to expect. I was really nervous, and I thought my legs would give out as I walked in. I can't give the disabilities team for Walker Stalker Con enough love—they are so, so good. While other conventions can be very difficult around disabilities, Walker Stalker Con goes out of its way to be accessible to all.

It was an amazing day from start to finish, even though it may sound like I didn't do much.

The first person I met was Tom Payne. I was so nervous I wanted to turn and run away. But when I saw him in real life, I had to take a moment. He is so pretty! I didn't really talk to him, I didn't have any words, but I got his autograph and a selfie. After that I headed to the quiet room and chilled out, while my dad made friends with the zombie cosplayers.

I'd booked a photo op with Tom Payne as well, so I got another chance to see him later in the afternoon. I asked for a hug and he gave me a huge one. It felt amazing to be able to meet someone I'd seen on television and admired hugely. It was over in about ten seconds, but I had the photo and the knowledge that I'd done it. It felt like such an achievement.

My favourite character on *The Walking Dead*, in common with many people, is Daryl Dixon (another broken soul to relate to, I suppose) and I also had a photo op booked with Norman Reedus, the actor who plays him. Doing that was properly terrifying. He was the main attraction and loads of people were queuing up. Those of us in the disability queue were anxiously chatting to one another as he was running about an hour late. Finally, though, the time came, and I walked in. Seeing him in real life was—I don't even have the words. Here was the man who had brought the character of Daryl to life, and although the photo op didn't give me the time to tell him that, I did get the biggest hug and I absolutely love the photo that came out. Afterwards, one of the girls I'd been talking to came up to me and told me that my photo op was really cute. I was thrilled with it and was already making plans to return the following year. Before I left, I got Chandler Riggs' autograph, which is worth its weight in gold now, if his queues this year are anything to go by. It was an amazing day.

In October of 2016, I attended the new and improved Nor-Con, held on a much bigger scale at the Norfolk Showgrounds. Loads of people were in cosplay and there were props to interact with and it was much more what I'd imagined a convention would be like. I got a photo on the Iron Throne (I've never watched Game of Thrones, but I couldn't resist) and my brother and I spent several happy hours pointing out people from different fandoms and admiring the costumes. We watched the cosplay competition in awe. It was a really great day and we promised each other we'd do it again the next year.

We did. This time I dressed up as a female Negan from *The Walking Dead*, complete with Lucille, his infamous baseball bat. My brother, his girlfriend and his friend dressed up as Team Rocket and found themselves being followed around by a Giovanni which freaked us all out a little when he called them his 'minions'.

I can't give enough praise to those who put conventions on, or indeed to those who cosplay or have stalls selling all kinds of geeky merchandise. The guests too—I know they make more money than god at these things, but it's worth it. I don't think they realise how much it means to a country bumpkin like myself to meet someone I've admired for years.

At Walker Stalker Con this year, I was lucky enough to meet Melissa McBride, who plays Carol Peletier in *The Walking Dead*, and was very nervous about being there. I told her how much her character meant to me, and she said, 'thank *you* for caring'. I also met Pollyanna McIntosh who plays Jadis, and whose storyline had me fascinated. I got a selfie with her. She looks great, me, less so. Finally, I met Tom Payne again. He was ill at the last con so hadn't been up to talking much, but this time he was fine, and I got a selfie and he was just lovely. Still so damn pretty.

I didn't have any photo ops this year, I couldn't afford it. Next year, though, I'm planning on getting loads. I also want to get the opportunity to meet Norman Reedus for longer than the five seconds a photo op takes to happen, something reserved for the higher tier tickets. I really hope I can, because I'd love to be able to tell him how much Daryl means to me, and to show him my Daryl-inspired tattoo. I did submit a piece to a fan book someone made for him, so hopefully he's seen it.

Fandom is an amazing, vibrant display of humanity's creativity and love and passion for the art of comics, television, movies and more. Sometimes it can bring out the worst in us, but ninety-nine per cent of the time, it brings us together. And I love it.

The gender and sexuality thing

2018

I almost decided not to write this essay. Like, I didn't need to tell you this, right? I didn't need to go into detail about the me that isn't immediately obvious. But then—that's kinda dishonest of me. I have an amazing amount of privilege in that I can pass as a cisgender straight woman in a world which is deeply unkind to anyone who strays outside of the gender or sexuality norms, and here I am, ignoring the fact that I am far, far from being either cis or straight.

Sexuality and gender are rarely discussed in relation to autism; I think a lot of people don't even realise that autistic people want or need relationships. Even programmes like *The Undateables* are weirdly sanitised, the autistic people chaperoned by their parents like they're going to their first school dance or something. There's something very childlike and infantilising about that, and it just rubs me up the wrong way.

So, cards on the table.

When I was in year two, I read the Famous Five books and watched the series based on them. I immediately fell in love with George, and for the first time in my life realised there was more to gender than what I'd been born into. I could *want* to be a boy, just like George did. Now, I've Googled, and there's very little out there about George being potentially the first children's transgender icon, but it was hugely important to me. I remember announcing to my friends (and anyone who would listen, really) at school, that when I grew up, I would be a boy. It just seemed obvious and easy. Like, no hurdles, no barriers, it would just be something I'd do, like dyeing my hair. Someone asked me if I'd have 'the surgery' and I was knocked back—wasn't it—I mean, couldn't I just *choose*?

I'd never been a girly girl, but after the revelation that girls could be boys and boys could be girls, and there was more to gender than my eight-year-old self could comprehend, I stopped wearing dresses and skirts and fell strictly into a more gender neutral aesthetic of fleeces (it was the nineties) and jeans. I wouldn't wear a skirt again until I was fifteen, and even then, it felt like playing dress-up. It still does, to be honest.

Around the same time, my girl friends were getting into boy bands. I...wasn't. I liked the Spice Girls and Steps and S Club 7 and Britney, but I couldn't name a boy band member if you paid me. I didn't get the appeal of men wandering around with their abs out at all. Whereas girls? Girls were awesome.

I sort of didn't think about it, I had other stuff going on. It's amazing how little you can think about such an important aspect of yourself when you're constantly anxious and throwing up a lot, and I managed to get through high school with only the vague feeling of 'well, something here is sort of off, but okay'.

Towards the end of high school, I'd been in fandom for a while and been drawn exclusively to male/male pairings, finding myself more able to relate to them than the straight pairings or female/female pairings. After getting past the initial ick factor (they put it *where*?!) it seemed a lot less gross to me than anything I personally had going on downstairs. Which was tricky.

Looking back, I love how naïve I was about everything. I honestly thought that when people talked about sex in movies or on television, in songs, the media, everything, that it was all a fiction, that nobody really believed it. People ruined their marriages for one-night stands? I couldn't understand it. I had never, ever had the drive or motivation to seek out anything close to that. Sure, I'd had crushes, but the idea of smooshing genitals with someone else? Please, god, no.

So, while everyone else was busy smooshing genitals, I read about fictional characters falling in love, scrolling past the genital smooshing parts, focusing on the slow realisation of feelings and repressed emotions. I liked the idea of love, but the idea of being obliged to sleep with someone else (in either sense, to be honest, I sleep like a wild animal, kicking and rolling around and generally acting very bizarrely indeed, so I don't think I'd make a good bed partner) disgusted me.

The thing about the internet, is that things evolved more slowly back then. And I evolved slowly with it. My Myspace page had a little button on it, a small piece of HTML that declared me 'straight but not narrow'. I didn't discriminate in who I thought was pretty by gender; I honestly never really thought about it at all until I watched *Skins*, a British

TV series which focused on teenage lives and would tackle issues affecting them.

She's in the very first episode, and she's beautiful. I didn't know if I wanted to be her or hold her hand (both, I think?) but she was like something I could have dreamt up if the gods of sleep were being particularly kind to me. Cassie Ainsworth was amazing. I wanted to rescue her, I wanted to be her, I wanted to help her recover. Even all these years later, I still refer to her as the love of my life. I have genuine mental crises over what I'd do if Cassie and Bucky showed up at my door at the same time, begging for my affections. I've never been able to make a decision.

And that's the famous joke about being bisexual, isn't it? Being unable to choose. But there was more to it than that, I was bisexual, sure, but I didn't want the sex bit. I thought it was kinda dumb at best. It sounded like it hurt and that it couldn't possibly be fun. I remember thinking the phrase 'lie back and think of England' a lot during that time, and whether that had been designed with me in mind.

Thankfully, my complete lack of allure prevented me from getting into a situation where sex would ever be an option. As someone with a potato for a face, I have been blessed as some kind of sexless being, by and large, and the whole ten-year-long hermit act has meant I've made it to twenty-nine years of age without even kissing anyone.

Which is handy, but lonely.

The word I found, eventually, was asexual. And I was, and am, completely and utterly, although it invites some fairly nasty comments and intrusive questions. It doesn't mean I'm not down for kissing or cuddling, but beyond that? I think I'd have to be with someone I really, really cared about, and it'd have to be for their benefit, and boundaries would have to be very firmly established. It's something I still think about a lot and beat myself up about. It does limit the dating pool significantly, because sex is a huge part of other people's lives. For me it's very abstract, like sky diving or swimming with sharks. Sure, do it if you want, but I'm going to stay home and *not*, if it's all the same to you.

The gender thing? That was something I didn't have words for until a couple of years ago. I'd never felt like I was a girl, but the idea of being a man, though tempting for numerous reasons, felt unrealistic, being that I was five foot two and generally very petite (not to disparage any petite trans men out there reading this, I'm sure you're freaking manly as hell and totally rock it). I sort of loved the idea of having facial hair but feared male pattern baldness. I didn't understand why life wasn't more like *The Sims* video game, where I could go to the mirror and just change what I looked like day by day. Because that's how I felt—mostly I felt in the middle, but some days I fell more on one side of the gender spectrum than the other.

I'd go through intense bouts of dysphoria, and self-hatred, throwing out all my gendered clothes and then regretting it a month later when I'd settled down again. My hair was long then short then long then short, and I still struggle with it because why on earth should the length of my hair be gendered?

My chest is small enough that I can get away with not wearing a bra unless I'm wearing something sheer or revealing (which is next to never, so), and I have a cheap binder I can put on if even that is too much. I've found that sometimes if I'm very lucky River Island will sell twenty-five inch men's jeans, which fit me so much better and more flatteringly than women's ever did. I'm lucky enough that my body type is naturally slim. I'm largely curveless, if you ignore my scoliosis.

The term I use for it is non-binary, which means I don't fit into the binary categories of male or female. It's part of the trans spectrum (there are many, many spectrums, gender, sexuality, autistic, the world is rarely as black and white as people try to make it).

If you looked at me, you probably wouldn't think I was anything other than a cisgendered straight woman. Which is extremely frustrating at times, because while dresses are fun sometimes, and makeup is fun too, it feels performative to me in a way that it shouldn't. I know that if I dress like a girl I get more attention online, if I act like a girl I get treated one way, whereas if I mention being non-binary I get the usual 'special snowflake' comments, which I think every millennial gets just for existing outside of the right-wing norms of conformity, or just a blank gaze. As someone who is older on the internet, and older in general now I come to think of it, I don't get the comments about it being a phase so much (bloody long phase, I'd have thought) and people online generally refer to me by they/them pronouns, which is something I long for in my everyday life but understand can be tricky to implement. While the grammar of it isn't wrong, it sounds wrong to someone who isn't used to it, and I don't think the world is quite there yet.

So, that was fun for me. Why did I tell you that? Because like I said, it doesn't get talked about. And while I don't want to boink anyone, other autistic people might want to. And I worry that just because they're autistic, they're not being considered as sexual beings in their own right, or indeed, gendered beings, and as such are being left out of important conversations.

Knowing who you are, discovering who you are, can take a lifetime. If you're never told about the options, if that sense of wrongness just settles within you, it can lead to a lifetime of torment. So I think it's important that we have this discussion, that we allow autistic people to exist on the various LGBT+ spectrums as well as the autistic one. It doesn't hurt anyone to acknowledge that that could be an option, and is, most likely, a reality.

Starstuff

2017

I don't know how I found out about the Spectrum Art Prize competition—designed to seek out autistic artists and celebrate what they can do and achieve. I think I just stumbled across it via some email about autism or another, some site had sent out a newsletter. It seemed like a really unique idea though, and I had a lot to say and this seemed like an opportunity to say it.

I didn't have the best equipment—a camera that didn't focus properly, a webcam in place of a microphone, and After Effects, a program I wasn't entirely sure how to use. The one thing I knew I could do was write. So, I started with that.

I opened a Notepad document, and just began to type. I started at the beginning—*you will be told you are a trouble-maker*. I remembered being in high school and my form teacher making phone calls to my mum. From there, the words flowed and before long I had my entire life story summed up in just over a thousand words. Some sentences hurt to type, like some of the sentences I've had to type writing this—*you will not be allowed to go home.*

I didn't want it to end on a negative though. I had to have hope, even if I hadn't believed in it at the time. I'd been to Walker Stalker Con the week before, you can see I'm still wearing the wristband in the video, and I was trying, really trying to be the person I knew I was supposed to be. So, in a way, 'How To Be Autistic' is as much a guide to me as it is to anybody watching.

I chose the title because I thought it was funny. There's no one way to be autistic, there are millions. Every autistic person is their own person with their own identity, and I wanted to get that message across. My experience is my experience. It might not have been yours. But we might have shared some of it.

I've always been fascinated by Carl Sagan's *Pale Blue Dot* monologue, where he describes how everyone you've ever known or heard of has had a home, a place on this planet, this strange spinning orb in space, that contains all our hopes and dreams and pasts and futures. I'd recommend looking it up, it's from the book *Pale Blue Dot: A Vision of the Human Future in Space.*

Another quote by Carl Sagan that has always grabbed me was more simple, more succinct—the fact that we are 'made of starstuff' (from *Cosmos*). This is a theme throughout popular culture, especially as we understand more and more about the big bang and how we are all made of the same elements that existed at the beginning of the universe and that will exist at the end of the universe too. We may not always take the same form, may not always be sentient or aware, but we will always exist in this universe until it doubles back on itself and creates a whole new universe. How many times has it done this? Millions? Billions? Once? How many lives have we lived, under a golden sun, starstuff thrumming in our veins?

I loved that from the first time I heard it. I really had a feeling of being absolutely tiny and absolutely huge at the same time. So mortal and ageless all at once. We are starstuff. We are exploded planets and we are all miracles. We have no way of knowing how many times a black hole has had to explode before we came along, before the stars aligned just right for us to exist.

The most important message though, was repeated throughout the poem I wrote, and it was simply this—*you will survive.* I was beginning to realise it, and I thought, well, if there's hope for me, there's going to be hope for other people as well. We have it hard, us autistic folk, the world isn't built for us, but we are, to quote myself, fucking cosmic. We are exceptional. We are one of a kind. And we will not be silenced.

After writing and editing the piece I recorded it on my webcam and played around with the audio as best I could in Audacity, trying to minimise the noise. Did you know that of the static you see on your television, 0.1 per cent of it is interference from the Big Bang? I know it's not the same, but it felt like a fitting tribute to leave the audio slightly imperfect, and similarly, the added grain to the film is another note to the universe.

Filming it was the hardest part. It was a single take, and I set up the tripod and just put myself back in the shoes of my fifteen-year-old self, with the hopelessness, the feeling of betrayal and lack of trust, the endless future, of being different and not knowing why, stretching out. I wore only my underwear because I wanted to be exposed. I didn't want to hide any part of me. I didn't want to distract. I just wanted to be on the camera, as a human being talking to another human being.

The final decision was to have the words HOW TO BE AUTISTIC splashed across the piece for the entire video. I wanted it to stand out, to be bold, to be a statement that couldn't be ignored. I wanted people to read it and want to know more.

I submitted the piece a few days later, and then, I waited. I waited for a long time. I thought it would be like when I'd submit my writing and never hear back, or receive a polite refusal.

I never expected to be shortlisted.

I never, in my wildest dreams, expected any of what followed.

I never, ever, expected to win.

Everything, everything

After I'd submitted my piece and mostly forgotten about it, I got on with my life. I was trying harder to go out more, especially to my ultimate nemesis—Tesco. It's the best of a bad lot of supermarkets for me, but it's still not a fun experience and I tend to struggle a lot with shopping. My mum will always go with me and give me the car keys so if I need to leave I can go sit in the car. But I was trying.

I also had a new nephew to help look after. In July, Roan Apollo joined his big brother, Ethan, and his big sister, Ella. He was the most alert baby I'd ever met, from day one his eyes would track you and you just knew there was someone in there. I've never met another baby like Roan. Having my nephews and niece has been a tremendous help to me. I have people to stick around for, and also, as they age, I need to be someone they look up to. It became hugely important to me that I was seen as someone they could be proud of. Maybe not in the same way other children are proud of their aunties, but I didn't want to be a deadbeat. I wanted to be there for them. I wanted to help them grow and thrive. So I had to let myself grow and thrive too.

Children really allow you to appreciate the passage of time and how quickly it falls through your cupped hands like water. I was edging ever closer to thirty and I'd achieved nothing. I wanted, in some small way, to make a difference. For too long, all my blog titles had been 'create something beautiful'. I wanted to do that. 'How To Be Autistic' was an attempt at that. So is this. There will be many more attempts. Creating something beautiful is not a finite goal, it is something based on purity and kindness and honesty, and I think that's what art is.

On 16 August 2017, I received an email saying I'd been shortlisted for the Spectrum Art Prize. I couldn't believe it. Just that afternoon my mum had gone to a charity to get help with filling in my benefits form while I'd sat at home stewing about how useless I was because I needed her to do that for me. And now here I was, being noticed. Being far from useless. There's no shame in needing benefits, but the media narrative is that there is, and if you're told something enough, you begin to believe it.

But this—receiving the email, being told that I would be visited and interviewed by Mary, the CEO of Spectrum, and Sacha, one of the art prize judges, and the idea of representing autistic people and our artwork—it felt so surreal. My mum still wasn't home, and I didn't know how to tell her. I hadn't told her about the film I'd made. I hadn't told anybody.

In the end, I sent a message via the family WhatsApp group, saying something along the lines of 'by the way, I think I've been shortlisted for an art prize.' My sister laughed when she read it. She'd come home with my mum after the benefit form-filling, and said 'well, I guess we needn't have done that.' But the future was far from certain and being shortlisted didn't mean I'd won. There was no chance I could actually win this thing, was there? I mean, I was me, and despite my best efforts my self-esteem was (and still is) shockingly low. There must be some mistake.

On 18 October, Mary and Sacha visited me. They were both so lovely, and I tried hard to answer their questions. I was honest, perhaps overly so, and spoke of not wanting anyone else to go through what I'd been through. I wanted to make a difference, be a resource. If my video could do that, then that would be all I could ask for. The prize itself was secondary. The message was everything. Art is the weapon.

On 19 December, a photographer came to take my photos for publicity. This was spiralling out of control at an alarming rate and I was along for the ride and loving it. For the first time it felt like I was truly alive, and I felt inspired, motivated, and while I knew I wouldn't win, I was just happy to be involved. Mary and Sacha had promised that even if I didn't win, I'd receive support from Spectrum, which meant I'd hopefully still be able to get my message out there.

On 19 March 2018, I received an email telling me that I was a finalist, and that my film would be exhibited in the Saatchi Gallery with the other six finalists' work.

I'd never even been to an art gallery before. Now I was going to be *in* one. I needed something to wear.

Finalist

2018

We travelled down to London on the Monday. The exhibition would open on the Tuesday night but there was some press planned for the morning at the Saatchi Gallery, so we had to be there bright-eyed and bushy-tailed.

My uncle has a flat in Shepherd's Bush which I frequently refer to as our AirBnB for all the times we've pitched him out of it over the years (not that many, to be fair, maybe three or four personally, but still). He taught me how to use Uber, and talked to me about how I was feeling, which was pretty damn nervous. I'd picked out an amazing dress which by sheer chance actually looked good on me, I have such bad luck with clothes, but my mum just took one look when I tried it on and said—'that's it, that's the one.' I had everything I would need, including a lot of diazepam because 'as needed' felt pretty damn needed right about now.

I did actually manage to get a little sleep on Monday night as, strangely for London, sirens weren't going off every five minutes and it was sort of quiet. I'd also discovered the secret to getting rid of the debilitating anxiety stomach cramps that had plagued me for years. Buscopan! My mum had recommended it and I'd tried it out of desperation. The tablets work so quickly—they're tiny miracle workers. Us autistic folk, we have to think outside of the box sometimes (well, we're already outside of the box, we're boxes upon boxes upon boxes).

On Tuesday morning I dressed in dungarees that made me look vaguely tall. I booked the Uber and before long me and my dad, who had travelled down to support me, were headed to the Saatchi Gallery. Not five minutes into the trip, the Uber was hit by a lorry and the wing mirror swiped. The Uber driver stopped the car and turned the hazards on and just ran after the lorry, leaving us sitting there wondering what on earth we were supposed to do next. He eventually came back, swearing and angry, which was fair enough I suppose. A couple of streets later we found the van parked up and details were exchanged, and we finally carried on to the gallery. (All the while my anxiety was building but in a very abstract way. There's a John Mulaney quote about adulthood that suits this situation which is 'this might as well happen'. I've been thinking that a lot lately!) We were early and the staff wouldn't let us in, so we sat in the sun in the grounds of the gallery and waited for it to open. We weren't there that long, and before I knew it we were meeting up with everyone from Spectrum and I got to see my work in a gallery for the very first time.

The room was gorgeously laid out, a big white space with all different kinds of artwork, a huge sculpture in the middle of the room, audio visual pieces (mine included) on three walls, and paintings taking up the remaining walls. It felt light and airy and in no way claustrophobic. I suddenly felt very middle class indeed.

I had to have some press photos taken, which was terrifying because I'm not a natural in front of the camera at all. You can find the stock images online and have a good laugh at my expense if you fancy it, I look like a deer in headlights. It didn't help that a few days before, a salon had ruined my eyebrows and I was feeling the loss.

Next, I had an interview with London Live, with a lovely man who asked me about my work. During the interview I thought about the good luck message my niece and nephew had sent me that morning, and it got me through. I tried to answer as eloquently as I could, and everyone watching said I did well.

(Don't you hate it when you've said or written something you can't take back and immediately think of ten better ways to say it? I've been doing that a lot lately too. I can only hope it gets easier with time.)

After that was all done, I had a good snoop around the other finalists' work. Any hope I had of winning all but vanished. They were all amazing, absolutely gorgeous, startling and bold. Mine felt unprofessional and mediocre in comparison, like a mistake or a kindness. I resigned myself to not winning. Being a finalist wouldn't necessarily be a bad thing—it's still an amazing accomplishment—but I think everyone kinda wants to win, right?

My mum would be getting the train at around 4pm, and we weren't due at the exhibition opening until 6pm, so we went back to my uncle's and I slept and my dad went and explored London. He's amazing like that, you can take him anywhere and when you're too exhausted or too anxious, he'll take himself off and find something to do. I envy that enormously.

My mum arrived safely, if a bit grumpy at my dad for

waiting for her on the wrong platform, and she reassured me that everything would be okay and that she was proud of me for getting this far. My mum, dad and uncle would all be going that night, as well as my friend Mervyn, who I mentioned all the way back in the college chapter.

Mervyn is amazing. He'll deny it, but he really, really is. I lost contact with him after college, and it was sheer chance that we started talking again. I hope he won't mind me admitting how I found him, but I was browsing OkCupid (hope springs eternal, right?) and there he was. I wrote him a kind of 'remember me?' message and he did, and before long we realised how much we had in common, and how we could have been friends for years, though maybe we had to be who we were when we started talking for that to be possible. I don't know, I don't believe in fate, but the stars definitely aligned when I stumbled across his profile. We started sending messages too long for OkCupid's ten-thousand-character limit and switched to email. That was about four or five years ago. We've been emailing ever since. That night though, would be the first time we'd seen each other in thirteen years. I was both excited and nervous—what if we didn't get on in real life? The night felt like a night of two huge events: finding out if I'd won (a very big deal) and meeting up with Mervyn (another very big deal).

The exhibition didn't open to the public until 7pm so we spent a lot of time hanging around and talking with everyone at Spectrum and looking at the art and trying to calm our nerves. I think everyone was a little nervous, except maybe my dad. He's never been nervous a day in his life.

At 7pm, people started to wander in, and before long the numbers were building and the room was filling. I texted Mervyn to ask if he was there yet. He replied saying he was, and I rushed to find him. And there he was—the same Mervyn I had known in college, the same Mervyn I had poured my heart out to in emails, standing there, and I just hugged him as hard as I could. In fact, I snuck in as many hugs as I could that night, and it still doesn't feel like enough.

We split up from my family and wandered around talking and looking at the art, trying to decipher it. What was far more puzzling, however, was the food, which was presented in terrariums and other things you'd find in a garden centre. I don't drink and neither does Mervyn, so we tried some awful fruit concoction which was immediately deemed a mistake. We passed on the opportunity to try the duck liver pate sticks. (If I ever had to organise an event about autism, I'd do what my sister did for her wedding reception and have several orders of pizza delivered. As I explained earlier, autistic people don't do well with new foods, and maybe the art world and London elite have very sophisticated palates, but I couldn't find anything to eat that night. Even my water had a piece of cucumber in it. It was all very strange.)

After an hour of the gallery getting more and more full, of talking and turning down food that looked like it should be on display rather than be eaten, the speeches began.

My stomach turned. Did this mean they'd be announcing the winner soon?

Sacha went around the room explaining each piece of art and why it had been chosen. I can't really remember what she said about mine, my memory of the entire night is sort of fragmented and hazy, but I assume she was complimentary (I mean, it'd be kinda weird if she wasn't, so yeah, we're going to go with complimentary). We saw an amazing performance by another finalist, and then Simon Baron-Cohen, one of the forefathers of research about autism, got up to speak about autism and the prize.

And then, it was time.

They didn't do the dramatic pause like on television, but it still felt like a lifetime.

'And the winner is…Charlotte Amelia Poe.'

My legs turned to jelly and the first thing I was aware of was my mum hugging me, and saying, 'you did it, you did it' and then Mervyn hugged me and everyone was clapping and I was just in shock. I couldn't take anything in, it felt so utterly surreal and dreamlike.

Many kind words were said about my film, about its rawness and honesty, but I could barely hear them. I just stood there, trying to take it in. I'd won. I'd actually won. This was going to change my life. After so much heartache and after letting everyone down so many times, I'd finally done something good. I wasn't just the person who hid away in their bedroom and wrote and hoped one day to be noticed—I had been noticed. It felt amazing.

So many people came up to congratulate me, and I didn't know what else to say but thank you, thank you, thank you. One judge told me it had been a unanimous vote, which felt insane to me. Part of me wanted to protest, but I squashed it down. I'd won. This wasn't a sympathy thing, they'd chosen me because they honestly thought I deserved it.

Mervyn kept repeating to me how much I deserved it, and I just couldn't keep the grin off my face. He was smiling hugely too. It just felt amazing.

I'd won.

That would take a lot of time to sink in.

In fact, it took nearly a week. I kept waking up in the middle of the night for days afterwards thinking it was the night before the exhibition, and that I'd dreamt the whole thing.

You've read my story. It's probably been a bit depressing in parts. It's certainly been depressing to live through. If you could have told six-year-old me, sixteen-year-old me, twenty-six-year-old me even, that I would win an art prize, that I would be an award-winning artist, that I would be in the Saatchi Gallery surrounded by people I love, making them proud, I wouldn't have believed you.

We left an hour later, me saying goodbye to Mervyn with another hug and wishing I could just take him home with me and went back to my uncle's flat. It felt like—I don't even know. Everyone was so elated. We started looking back on the evening to see if there was any way we could have predicted it, but there hadn't been.

The world had become stranger than I'd previously been aware of, more wonderful still. And it was only the beginning.

Eyes in the sky

2018

Winning felt so far removed from anything I'd ever experienced, and also felt like a definite middle finger to all those people who had written me off or called me a troublemaker.

So many people had seen my film. Had heard its words. I could only hope that it would help.

The PR manager phoned and said that Sky News wanted to interview me and Charming Baker, one of the judges, live that afternoon. After a lot of negotiating we agreed a time. I hadn't slept the night before, and had snuck an hour in that afternoon, waking up feeling like death as you do sometimes after a nap you shouldn't have taken. I wanted to go home. I hadn't been away from home for so long since camp in middle school, and I'd hated it then and I was beginning to get antsy about it now. But Sky News? I couldn't refuse.

I wore my Keaton Henson t-shirt because he's always inspired me. I've always said, if I had one tenth of the talent he has in his little finger I'd be happy. (He's a musician, an artist, a composer, a poet, a writer, he's a genius. I'd love to meet him someday and just thank him, though I'd never be able to find the words.) He'd inspired me to write, and I often listened to his music while doing so. It felt like a fitting tribute.

They sent a car for me (I was getting cars called for me— my life had flip-turned upside down for good) and on the way to the studio my dad sat beside me, talking nonsense at me as I'd requested, to take my mind off the fact I'd be speaking live in front of millions of people. My mum and uncle would be at the flat watching it on television.

The second we got out of the car, rain started bucketing down with huge heavy droplets soaking us to the bone. We passed through security and ran to the building, which was as far away from the car park as you could get. By the time we'd got there and signed in, we looked like drowned rats. Charming met us there, and he and Dad had a coffee while I wondered what on earth I was going to do or say. I *really* didn't want to vomit on Kay Burley.

Before long, the runner came to get us and take us to the green room, where I was hustled into the hair and makeup section and let me tell you, if I had the money, I would hire a professional makeup artist to follow me around every day. I totally get it now. She dried and styled my hair, did my makeup beautifully (I don't normally do makeup at all, so it was like seeing a different person), she even managed to get eyeliner on me (I'm really funny about people going anywhere near my eyes, I can't even curl my own eyelashes). By the time she was finished I looked like a different person. She'd even fixed my eyebrows.

Next, we had to be micced up, I had been worried about that but had got to used to the idea by that point. I was literally vibrating with nerves, and if you watch the interview, you'll notice Kay points out that I'm shaking right at the beginning.

We were told how things would work, that there would be a thirty second interval when we had to get on set and into our chairs, and that once it was over, we weren't to move until we were told to.

The second I was out there, I completely forgot about anyone watching. They had been supposed to prep us for the questions but because they were running late there hadn't been time. And they were hard questions. I stumbled through as best I could, with Charming and Kay both rescuing me more than once. It felt like watching University Challenge—I knew I could get the answer if I could just have a few more seconds to think about it.

It was over before I knew it. Kay asked if we'd like a selfie, which we did, and then I was un-micced and we were sent on our way. I was in a daze, I couldn't remember a thing I'd said, and only hoped I'd done okay.

A car was waiting to pick us up and take us back to my uncle's, and my mum was waiting for me, she'd texted me and told me I'd done well. She told me she could never have done it, which puzzled me, as I thought neurotypical people could just do stuff like that? I guess I still have a lot to learn.

We set off home to avoid the rush hour, but we hit gridlock anyway. It took an hour and a half to get out of London proper, and then we didn't get home until 9.30pm. I was so tired I just wanted to sleep for about a million years. I was also hungry. Anxiety doesn't exactly give you permission to eat.

When we got home, I got to watch the Sky interview for the first time. I cringed at every sentence fragment I didn't manage to complete, but I didn't do too terribly, I thought.

And for the first time in my life, I thought I actually looked bordering on pretty.

I know I keep saying it, but it felt surreal to watch it, like watching somebody else. I couldn't believe that a week ago I'd been helping to babysit my littlest nephew, and then that day I'd been on Sky News.

Spectrum rang and congratulated me, saying I did really well. I wasn't so sure about that, but I think I did okay. And I'd managed to mention the thing you're holding now, all things going according to plan, which was the book I'd wanted to write for years—the story of how to be autistic.

better

i read a line in a book recently
that said 'this is what better looks like for me'
and better wasn't really best it was more like surviving
than thriving
you see—
sometimes you don't get to choose the path less travelled
or even the path with handy signposts and friendly guides
sometimes it's hard enough to reach the starting line
let alone to ramble
while others wade through mud and rivers
filling their boots with cold and wet
laughing at nature and how the world makes them feel alive
there are those of us who stay inside
and start to forget the sun on their skin
or the way it felt to meet somebody new without pretence or
    expectation
when the noise overwhelms
and there's too much to see
because the world is sharp edges, too much for me
when late night car rides and half hour conversations
are as much as this muddled brain can bear
when you look for me and find that i'm not there
when you cut a hole inside my chest and tunnel past my spine
and i ask if you can see through me now
as i bleed this unholy wine
you don't reply because you finally see
this is what better looks like for me.

Better

When I first started writing this book, I had a lot of ideas about what I wanted to say, about how I wanted to depict my life. It's easy to think these things, and much harder to put them down on paper. I don't want anyone to think that what happened to me is an inevitability, or that autism is the end of the world. It's not, it's really not.

It's hard to be positive sometimes. I know I lost a lot of years to the inertia of just being, without course, without any sense of direction. And I hate that. I hate that I didn't get to go to university. I hate that I failed school so spectacularly. I hate that I don't have a solid group of friends or a partner I can rely on. I hate that I still live at home.

But I've gotten better than I was. The self-loathing stems from years of being told I was worthless or difficult—and that's hard to get over, especially without help. Even now, I feel like a fraud, like I somehow cheated and tricked everyone with the Spectrum Art Prize. I entered it because I had something to say, not because I considered myself an artist. I just wanted to tell my story and hope that someone

145

heard. I never thought I'd win. Everything that has followed has left me utterly bewildered and I really don't know what to tell you—I tried to create something beautiful, at a point where I was turning my life around in tiny, incremental ways, and it sort of got away from me.

There are some people who are just naturally extremely engaging and talented. And then there's me. When I'm interviewed, my mum always tells me to be myself. 'But that's the worst person I could be!' I reply. I don't think I'm joking.

I'm trying hard to put the past in the past and writing this book has been cathartic in that way, but it's something I have to carry with me as well. If you gave me a time machine, there's a lot I would change, but then I worry, what would I stand to lose by doing so? Would I still get to have my nephews and niece? My cats? If I change the past, do I lose the good things about the now?

My eldest nephew is a spitfire and a dervish all at once. He's so clever. And he knows it. He doesn't question that he knows everything. But he's also one of the kindest human beings I've ever met, he is completely non-judgemental, and doesn't want me to be anybody but myself.

My niece is sunshine, pure bottled sunshine. She lacks the confidence of her older brother. She's just as smart, but she doesn't believe it quite so much. She's a princess, but the type of princess you'd read about in a story, who works hard for her fairy-tale ending. And she's just as kind and thoughtful as her brother, just as vibrant.

My youngest nephew is only ten months old as I write this but is already part of my saving grace. I've never really gelled with babies all that well, they're too breakable, and too often just not 'there' enough to really connect with. But he was there from the moment he opened his eyes. He's the most destructive, demanding force in my life, he takes up so much of my time, and I feel honoured that he allows me that. I was afraid when he was born that I wouldn't be a part of his life, that I couldn't love him enough, but I do love him, and I get to see him almost every day.

How could I go back in time and risk losing them?

Time is cruel, because it gives and takes. Who I am now is moulded on who I was five years ago, ten years ago, twenty years ago. I am everything that has happened to me. I can't change that. I can change how I think and feel and respond to that, but I can't change the building blocks of myself.

I have to come to terms with that, as hard as it feels. It's not easy. In the same way you don't just snap out of depression, you can't just snap out of post traumatic stress disorder (PTSD) and all it entails. The nightmares don't just go away, the moments when you're sitting and suddenly you're back there, right back there, just for a few seconds, before you're back in the present, and it feels so real—that doesn't go away. The anxiety, the depression, every defence your body and brain have built up to protect you—the distrust of authority and the rebel nature of your soul, you can't just shut those off because the danger has passed.

When you survive something, whether it be prolonged trauma from growing up and being treated like something on the bottom of someone's shoe, over and over again, or whether it's just one big trauma, it doesn't matter what it was—it's still valid. We, as a society, like to compare pains and mental anguishes as though one can somehow trump another. But your pain is your pain, and if it is hurting you, then it matters. Don't compare yourself to somebody else, just compare yourself to yourself. Day to day, hour to hour.

If you feel like you're at risk, tell someone. If you feel slightly better, count it as a win. I know it's a cliché and oft repeated, but it really does get better. And I know the resources aren't out there. I know. But you've made it through everything so far, and you're still standing. That's absolutely incredible, you know that?

It took everything I had to function at school, and it still takes everything I have to talk to people now. I don't know if that'll ever really change. How hard everything is. All the time. But I can say subjectively, at least, that it's better than it was. It's really dumb, but it's true, living a happy life after trauma really is the biggest fuck you that you can give to the person or people who hurt you.

Writing the script for 'How To Be Autistic', I think I was hoping they'd see it—all the people who told me I was worthless, who called me a troublemaker. I wanted them to see it and realise what they'd done, both good and bad. They'd made me stronger, but they'd also pushed me to breaking point. I shouldn't have had to go through that. I'm sure you're thinking of things you shouldn't have had to go through too.

Living well is the best revenge, right? Well, we don't all get the opportunity or have the privilege to live well, but we can live as best we can. There's pleasure in the small things, and I think we forget that. If we allow ourselves to become fixed, to become numb to the world, we forget how to feel. I know, because I did. Depression isn't something you can pep talk yourself out of, much as that'd be nice, neither is anxiety, but there are ways of coping, ways of making it not so bad. There are a thousand blogs and videos online dedicated to mental health, and hundreds of charities who want to help you live your best life.

Better

It turns out I needed four things—my niece and nephews, and a miracle. My miracle was the Spectrum Art Prize, and it was a bolt from the blue. I can't tell you what your miracle will be, and it's not a miracle in any god-shaped way, it's just a fluke, something that'll happen because the universe is weirder than we can possibly imagine. Sometimes you have to chase after it. Sometimes it'll just come to you. If I've learnt anything from this whole thing, it's to chase opportunities. If you create art in any form, there are thousands of online zines that are looking for you and will pay you for your work. There are competitions all the time. There are cafes looking to display local artists' work.

And if you feel like you really can't create anything, well, you're wrong. I know you can. Art isn't inherently good or bad, or ugly or beautiful, it's honest. The next chapter will talk more about that, but anyone can make art. Art doesn't discriminate by class or creed, making marks on paper is something nearly anyone can do. If Jackson Pollock can sip vodka and drizzle paint, who on earth can tell you that what you create is any less worthy? Any less valuable?

What is getting better? I don't know. It's a process. It's looking back on where you were six months ago and not knowing that person any more. It's wondering if you'd recognise yourself if you went back to you at ten years old and told them who you'd be, what you've accomplished.

By birth, we were handed a rather poor hand. But by continuing to fight, every damn day, in a world that is not ours and is not shaped to handle us, we show how strong we are, and every second we're breathing is in utter defiance of everyone who ever told us we were wrong.

Please don't give up.

Who tells our stories?

Who tells the stories of autistic people? Ninety-nine per cent of the time, it's neurotypical people—neurotypical authors, neurotypical scientists, neurotypical voiceovers. It's their narratives we are forced to conform to, and their narratives the public sees.

This is my narrative. This is a book by an autistic person, and it isn't just for autistic people, but for everyone. It's not fair that we are silenced, that there are autism charities without a single autistic member on the board, that we are spoken over time and time again. Think about the television programme *The Undateables* and how the footage is manipulated to make us seem foolish and inept. Compare it to a similar programme, *First Dates*, where ineptitude isn't mocked but seen as human, or at worst, boring. We are othered at every turn, we are seen as something other than human. We are a puzzle piece, needing to be solved.

Are we though? Or are we more than that? Are we not, instead, all individuals with our own unique abilities, just like everybody else? Are we not strong and brave and magnificent in our own right? Sometimes, we may not be able to find our words, but that doesn't mean they should be replaced by somebody else's.

People are aware of autism in the same way they're aware of house fires: both are scary things that happen to other people. But as more people seek diagnosis and more people are successfully diagnosed, it's time for society to realise that it could happen to you, or to someone you love. And that people with autism are not scary. Our lives are only made terrifying to us by the forces put in our way, by the people who don't understand, by overwhelming environments that don't cater to our unique ways of viewing the world.

Think, for a moment, about whether you know someone who wears glasses or contact lenses. Of course you do. But imagine if being long- or short-sighted was seen as the disability it actually is, if it was treated with stigma and people didn't receive help for it. Imagine people being unable to work because they couldn't see well enough to drive, cross the road or use a computer. Imagine a world where 'an epidemic of short-sightedness swept the nation'.

But it's not like that, is it? There's a Specsavers in every high street. This is a disability that is catered to, glasses are available to anybody, check-up reminders are slipped through letterboxes.

I'm not asking for a high street presence for people with autism, but I am asking for more than we've got. Just because you can't *see* autism, doesn't make it any less of a disability than any other. We struggle every day. We're made to feel like burdens. We're put into homes. We're put on waiting lists. We're bullied and mocked and laughed at by the media.

We are worth more than this. We are human beings. Our skills are valuable. Our ways of thinking are valuable.

Just give us room to breathe and a few accommodations and watch us go. There are those of us who are utterly reliant on other people, this is true, but even they shouldn't be written off as less than. There's a person inside there, even if you personally can't find them. And they're looking out, and your world is just as confusing to them as theirs is to you.

To neurotypical people reading this: it's time to do your bit. You've raised awareness, that's great, we're all aware of autism now. But what's your next step? We need action, not fearmongering. Train more people to diagnose and recognise autism. Prepare not just for autistic children but for autistic adults. Make it so that putting autism on your resume isn't an automatic veto. Make the Autism Act 2009 a thing that actually stands up and people are aware of. Allow us to be part of society on our terms. Don't write us off when you haven't given us a chance.

To autistic people out there reading this: I hope this book has helped in some way. Maybe you've recognised a piece of yourself in what I've written. Maybe it's angered you. Maybe it's helped you to make peace with a part of yourself. I never had a book like this to read growing up. Maybe if I had, things would have been very different.

Finding yourself in popular culture is invaluable. We need to be seen. And we're not, or at least, not in the way we should be. We should be the ones talking when someone needs a soundbite about the struggles autistic people face. We should be seen as just as valuable a resource for autism research as scientists and doctors. We may not be trained, but we have the life experience and we are autism.

It's hard. It's incredibly hard. Writing this has reminded me of how hard it was for me, and how hard it still is. I'm not cured, my anxiety and depression and PTSD are all still there. I can manage them with medication but it's not a fix-it. And I'll always be autistic. So many charities rage against that, wasting so much money looking for a cure. And I understand that, to a point—they're afraid of us, they're afraid for their children. We've been made out to have one of the worst disorders you can get. Utterly incurable and utterly alien.

Well, I say, fuck that. We are our brains and our brains are autistic. And it's time people accept that. We need to be heard. We need to create. We need to do what we're best at. We need to use our talents and change the world. I know rallying autistic people is like herding cats, we're all so unique, but that's what makes us amazing, we have an entire spectrum to draw from and each of us has a different voice.

Create something beautiful. Write a blog post. Make a Youtube video. Paint something. Sing. Dance. Anything. Everything. *It doesn't have to be perfect*. Art isn't about being perfect, it's about being authentic. It's about making people feel.

I know we've got a lot to say and I think it's about time we said it.

I'm going to leave you now, and I want to thank you for reading this far. For me, this is the beginning of a beginning. I hope it is for you too. You will survive. You will. I promise.

After all, **you are fucking cosmic.**

Acknowledgements

I have so many people to thank for making this book happen. Firstly, to my mum, for teaching me to love books and for telling me I could be whatever I wanted to be (it was always a writer). Thank you for being so patient and for living through all those bad years with me. Nothing I say could ever be thanks enough for everything you've done for me, and continue to do for me, every single day. It is an honour to have you as a mum, and I am so, so grateful to you.

To my dad, who gets dragged along to all the conventions even though he doesn't understand them, and who supports me unconditionally through all my hare-brained schemes and ideas. You instilled a love and understanding of music in me that I am so thankful for.

To my sister, Rosie, for being so kind and generous with me despite the difficult years. I know it hasn't been easy, but it's been a privilege to watch you grow and develop into a beautiful, intelligent woman with a wonderful family. I am so proud of you.

To my brother, Joe, who is kind and generous and, annoyingly, much taller than I am. Again, I am so proud of you for all you've accomplished, and I know you will achieve great things.

To my nephew, Ethan, who has taught me so much and whose passion for knowledge and intense curiosity inspire me every day. One day you will write an epic series of books, and I want the first signed copy.

To my niece, Ella, who is a constant bright light even on the dark days, who is full of magic and creativity. It is a joy and a pleasure to be invited into your stories, and it is nice to know that the ability to not sit properly is indeed genetic.

To my nephew, Roan, who has taught me more about being an adult than anyone else ever could, while at the same time allowing me to be carefree and dance to Baby Shark (on repeat) and to genuinely enjoy just existing with you. You're a complete mischief and I adore you for it.

To my littlest nephew, Remi, the tiniest human. I look forward to getting to know you and who you are.

To my uncle, Mikey, thank you for letting us kick you out of your flat every time we come up to London. Thank you also for telling me about your travels, and for showing me you never have to truly grow up.

To Mervyn, who has been the lighthouse in the storm for the past few years now, and who believes in me in a way few others could. I am so honoured to call you my best friend, and you inspire me to be a better person. Thank you for late night emails and for being there. I owe you so much.

Thank you to Mary from Spectrum, for being my fairy godmother and for believing in this book and, more importantly, for believing in me. You do such amazing work, and I've told you before, but I'll say it again, winning the Spectrum Art Prize was life-changing for me, and I can never repay that.

Acknowledgements

Thank you to Sacha, for helping me get this book to the right people and for being so kind and lovely.

To Corinne and Candida at Myriad Editions, for deciding to publish this book, and for making a childhood dream a reality. Thank you for your kind words, and for all the work you've done. Thank you also to my editor, Dawn, who made *How To Be Autistic* legible. And my cover designer, Clare, who I probably drove half-mad with my demands!

To everyone in the fandom, the fic writers and fanartists, to the people who have commented on my work and supported me, who have boosted me up and allowed me to believe in my writing. It's been an honour serving with you.

To Hozier, Keaton Henson, dodie and Panic! At The Disco for being the musical accompaniment for this book.

And finally, to Laura, for talking to me about writing; to Julie, for being a tumblr friend; to Jo, for inspiring many a poem; to Amber, Sophia and Mischa, for being the best damn cats; to John Green, whose advice was invaluable ('give yourself permission to suck and get the words on the page'); to James Buchanan (Bucky) Barnes, for being fictional but nonetheless the most inspiring character I've ever seen on page or screen; to everyone who has interviewed me; to everyone who has contacted me; to everyone who has taken time out of their day to read my dumb tweets or comment on my Instagram.

And thank you, dear reader, to you. A book is an object, it is only when it is opened and read that it becomes real. So, thank you for reading, right to the very end. You don't know how much this means to me, and I am eternally grateful.

Sign up to our mailing list at
www.myriadeditions.com
Follow us on Facebook and Twitter

About the author

Charlotte Amelia Poe is a self-taught artist and writer from Suffolk. She also works with video, and won the inaugural Spectrum Art Prize with the spoken word piece 'How To Be Autistic'.